OPPOSING
VIEWPOINTS®
SERIES

Internet Censorship

Other Books of Related Interest:

Opposing Viewpoints Series

Hacking and Hackers

Mass Media

Netiquette and Online Ethics

At Issue Series

Location-Based Social Networking and Services

What Is the Impact of Twitter?

Current Controversies Series

E-books

Internet Activism

Mobile Apps

"Congress shall make no law ... abridging the freedom of speech, or of the press."

First Amendment to the US Constitution

The basic foundation of our democracy is the First Amendment guarantee of freedom of expression. The Opposing Viewpoints Series is dedicated to the concept of this basic freedom and the idea that it is more important to practice it than to enshrine it.

OPPOSING
VIEWPOINTS®
SERIES

Internet Censorship

Margaret Haerens and Lynn M. Zott, Book Editors

GREENHAVEN PRESS
A part of Gale, Cengage Learning

GALE
CENGAGE Learning·

Farmington Hills, Mich • San Francisco • New York • Waterville, Maine
Meriden, Conn • Mason, Ohio • Chicago

Elizabeth Des Chenes, *Director, Content Strategy*
Cynthia Sanner, *Publisher*
Douglas Dentino, *Manager, New Product*

For more information, contact:
Greenhaven Press
27500 Drake Rd.
Farmington Hills, MI 48331-3535
Or you can visit our Internet site at gale.cengage.com

For product information and technology assistance, contact us at

Gale Customer Support, 1-800-877-4253
For permission to use material from this text or product, submit all requests online at www.cengage.com/permissions

Further permissions questions can be emailed to permissionrequest@cengage.com

Articles in Greenhaven Press anthologies are often edited for length to meet page requirements. In addition, original titles of these works are changed to clearly present the main thesis and to explicitly indicate the author's opinion. Every effort is made to ensure that Greenhaven Press accurately reflects the original intent of the authors. Every effort has been made to trace the owners of copyrighted material.

Cover image copyright © Images.com/Corbis.

LIBRARY OF CONGRESS CATALOGING-IN-PUBLICATION DATA

Internet censorship / Margaret Haerens and Lynn M. Zott, book editors.
    pages cm. -- (Opposing viewpoints)
    Includes bibliographical references and index.
    ISBN 978-0-7377-6658-5 (hardcover) -- ISBN 978-0-7377-6659-2 (pbk.)
    1. Internet--Censorship. I. Haerens, Margaret, editor of compilation. II. Zott, Lynn M. (Lynn Marie), 1969- editor of compilation.
    ZA4201.I554 2014
    025.042--dc23
                                                            2013035539

Printed in the United States of America
  2 3 4 5 6   19 18 17 16 15

Contents

Chapter 3: What Are the Best Ways to Fight Internet Censorship?

Chapter 4: Which Legal Measures Effectively Address Internet Censorship?

Why Consider
Opposing Viewpoints?

"The only way in which a human being
can make some approach to knowing the
whole of a subject is by hearing what
can be said about it by persons of every
variety of opinion and studying all
modes in which it can be looked at by
every character of mind. No wise man
ever acquired his wisdom in any mode
but this."

John Stuart Mill

In our media-intensive culture it is not difficult to find differing opinions. Thousands of newspapers and magazines and dozens of radio and television talk shows resound with differing points of view. The difficulty lies in deciding which opinion to agree with and which "experts" seem the most credible. The more inundated we become with differing opinions and claims, the more essential it is to hone critical reading and thinking skills to evaluate these ideas. Opposing Viewpoints books address this problem directly by presenting stimulating debates that can be used to enhance and teach these skills. The varied opinions contained in each book examine many different aspects of a single issue. While examining these conveniently edited opposing views, readers can develop critical thinking skills such as the ability to compare and contrast authors' credibility, facts, argumentation styles, use of persuasive techniques, and other stylistic tools. In short, the Opposing Viewpoints Series is an ideal way to attain the higher-level thinking and reading skills so essential in a culture of diverse and contradictory opinions.

In addition to providing a tool for critical thinking, Opposing Viewpoints books challenge readers to question their own strongly held opinions and assumptions. Most people form their opinions on the basis of upbringing, peer pressure, and personal, cultural, or professional bias. By reading carefully balanced opposing views, readers must directly confront new ideas as well as the opinions of those with whom they disagree. This is not to simplistically argue that everyone who reads opposing views will—or should—change his or her opinion. Instead, the series enhances readers' understanding of their own views by encouraging confrontation with opposing ideas. Careful examination of others' views can lead to the readers' understanding of the logical inconsistencies in their own opinions, perspective on why they hold an opinion, and the consideration of the possibility that their opinion requires further evaluation.

Evaluating Other Opinions

To ensure that this type of examination occurs, Opposing Viewpoints books present all types of opinions. Prominent spokespeople on different sides of each issue as well as well-known professionals from many disciplines challenge the reader. An additional goal of the series is to provide a forum for other, less known, or even unpopular viewpoints. The opinion of an ordinary person who has had to make the decision to cut off life support from a terminally ill relative, for example, may be just as valuable and provide just as much insight as a medical ethicist's professional opinion. The editors have two additional purposes in including these less known views. One, the editors encourage readers to respect others' opinions—even when not enhanced by professional credibility. It is only by reading or listening to and objectively evaluating others' ideas that one can determine whether they are worthy of consideration. Two, the inclusion of such viewpoints encourages the important critical thinking skill of objectively evaluating an author's credentials and bias. This evaluation will illuminate an author's reasons for taking a particular stance on an issue and will aid in readers' evaluation of the author's ideas.

It is our hope that these books will give readers a deeper understanding of the issues debated and an appreciation of the complexity of even seemingly simple issues when good and honest people disagree. This awareness is particularly important in a democratic society such as ours in which people enter into public debate to determine the common good. Those with whom one disagrees should not be regarded as enemies but rather as people whose views deserve careful examination and may shed light on one's own.

Thomas Jefferson once said that "difference of opinion leads to inquiry, and inquiry to truth." Jefferson, a broadly educated man, argued that "if a nation expects to be ignorant and free . . . it expects what never was and never will be." As individuals and as a nation, it is imperative that we consider the opinions of others and examine them with skill and discernment. The Opposing Viewpoints Series is intended to help readers achieve this goal.

David L. Bender and Bruno Leone,
Founders

Introduction

"The benefits of the open and accessible Internet are nearly incalculable and their loss would wreak significant social and economic damage."

Vinton Cerf,
"Keep the Internet Open,"
New York Times, May 24, 2012

On June 10, 2013, US district court judge Jesse Furman revived a lawsuit filed by pro-democracy activists against China and Baidu, China's most widely used Internet search engine. Initially filed in May 2011, the lawsuit alleges that China and Baidu conspired to suppress the political speech of the plaintiffs, eight writers and video producers based in New York City, by removing their work from the Internet search engine. By allowing the lawsuit to go forward, Judge Furman also opened the door for a larger dialogue on China's censorship of the Internet and its contentious relationship with Baidu's main competitor in China—Google, the massively popular and powerful US Internet company.

Google's relationship with China began in 2006, when the company launched a Chinese version of the search engine that was subject to the country's stringent censorship rules. In China, Internet content is rigorously censored: users are blocked from accessing dissenting ideological and political information; websites for pro-democracy groups, the Tibetan independence movement, and banned spiritual movements like the Falun Gong are hacked and disabled; "vulgar" and explicit sites and blogs are closed; and private communications between activists are disrupted and blocked by Chinese officials. Furthermore, political activists and members of outlawed groups are identified, closely monitored, investigated, and even jailed. China's control over the Internet within its borders is regarded as the most extensive and effective in the world.

In the first few years of doing business in China, Google was largely willing to self-censor content according to China's authoritarian censorship practices. The free world's reaction to Google's actions was sharp. Civil libertarians, human rights activists, political commentators, and government officials excoriated Google and other American companies willing to allow censorship in order to do business with China. The US House Subcommittee on Africa, Global Human Rights, and International Operations called for hearings on the matter in February 2006. Representative Tom Lantos read a statement regarding the role of Google and Yahoo in China: "These companies need to do more than show they have virtual backbone. What Congress is looking for is real spine and a willingness to stand up to the outrageous demands of a totalitarian regime. . . . They need to stand with us in fighting repression in China and everywhere they intend to do business."[1]

Elliot Schrage, vice president of global communications and public affairs at Google, responded to the backlash against his company and others at the hearings. "At the outset, I want to acknowledge what I hope is obvious: Figuring out how to deal with China has been a difficult exercise for Google," he stated. "The requirements of doing business in China include self-censorship—something that runs counter to Google's most basic values and commitments as a company. Despite that, we made a decision to launch a new product for China— Google.cn—that respects the content restrictions imposed by Chinese laws and regulations. Understandably, many are puzzled or upset by our decision. But our decision was based on a judgment that Google.cn will make a meaningful— though imperfect—contribution to the overall expansion of access to information in China."[2]

In May 2009, Google's precarious relationship with China began to unravel when the Chinese government blocked the video-sharing network YouTube over a video that purportedly shows Chinese security forces brutally beating Tibetan protesters in 2008. For many years, China's treatment of Tibet has been a matter of global controversy: Tibetans regard China's rule as an occupation and accuse Chinese forces of viciously oppressing the Tibetan people and culture; China contends that Tibet has always been rightfully considered a part of China and that Tibetan leaders are exaggerating human rights abuses to garner support from the West.

Chinese officials underscored the need to regulate the Internet in the wake of censoring YouTube, which is owned by Google. "China's Internet is open enough, but also needs to be regulated by law in order to prevent the spread of harmful information and for national security,"[3] said Qin Gang, a foreign ministry spokesman, to reporters.

In January 2010, Google announced that it would stop censoring Internet search results in China as a result of a cyberattack launched on the company by Chinese hackers. Company officials suggested that the attack was aimed to gather information on Chinese human right activists. Attacks were also perpetrated on a number of other US-based Internet social media and web-browsing companies, including Facebook, Twitter, and YouTube.

Google acknowledged that this move could mean the end of doing business in China. In a statement on the company's blog, Google official David Drummond asserted: "These attacks and the surveillance they have uncovered—combined with the attempts over the past year to further limit free speech on the web—have led us to conclude that we should review the feasibility of our business operations in China. We have decided that we are no longer willing to continue censoring our results on Google.cn, and so over the next few weeks we will be discussing with the Chinese government the basis on which we could operate an unfiltered search engine within the law, if at all. We recognize that this may well mean having to shut down Google.cn, and potentially our offices in China."[4]

On March 23, 2010, Google took further action, automatically redirecting all search requests from Google.cn to Google.com.hk, which is based in Hong Kong. This move allowed the company to provide uncensored results to users within China, because the Hong Kong site was not subject to Chinese censorship practices. After China banned Google search sites in retaliation, Google relented and ended the automatic redirect.

In May 2012, Google announced that it would offer a notification message to Chinese users when they search for controversial phrases or keywords that they might experience connection problems (The message: "In accordance with local laws, regulations and policies, part of the search result is not shown."). It also suggested alternative words for better search results. Chinese officials blocked the notification twice before Google decided to drop it altogether in May 2013, citing concerns over user experience. For many observers, Google's decision to eliminate the notification message signaled a capitulation to China and its tightening Internet censorship practices.

Google's experience in China reflects the growing concern over Internet censorship and the controversy over Internet sovereignty. The authors of the viewpoints presented in *Opposing Viewpoints: Internet Censorship* debate these issues within the following chapter headings: Should the Internet Be Censored?, Who Should Govern the Internet?, What Are the Best Ways to Fight Internet Censorship?, and Which Legal Measures Effectively Address Internet Censorship? The information in this volume will provide insight into recent controversies, including the dangers of government regulation of the Internet, who should have the power to govern the Internet, and emerging technologies, legislation, and diplomatic efforts that aim to protect Internet freedom in the United States and all over the world.

Notes

1. Tom Lantos, "Statement Regarding Internet Freedom in China," Lantos Foundation for Human Rights and Justice, January 15, 2010. www.lantosfoundation.org/news/News2010/2010_January_15-1.asp.

2. Elliot Schrage, "Testimony of Google Inc. before the Subcommittee on Asia and the Pacific, and the Subcommittee on Africa, Global Human Rights, and International Operations, Committee on International Relations, United States House of Representatives," *Google Official Blog*, February 15, 2006. http://googleblog.blogspot.com/2006/02/testimony-internet-in-china.html.

3. Quoted in Tania Branigan, "China Blocks YouTube," *The Guardian* (Manchester, UK), March 25, 2009.

4. David Drummond, "A New Approach to China," *Google Official Blog*, January 12, 2010. http://googleblog.blogspot.com/2010/01/new-approach-to-china.html.

OPPOSING
VIEWPOINTS®
SERIES

CHAPTER 1

Should the Internet Be Censored?

Chapter Preface

In the wake of the 2010 WikiLeaks scandal, a global debate erupted over issues of government secrecy and national security, the treatment of whistleblowers, and challenges of protecting classified information in a networked world. From the beginning, WikiLeaks set out to be a way for whistleblowers to bring information to the public. Since its launch, WikiLeaks has published thousands of documents and videos sent by anonymous whistleblowers that have sparked governmental and journalistic investigations as well as criminal prosecutions. Many of these leaks cast a bright light on the corruption and human rights abuses of repressive and secretive regimes in Asia, Africa, and the Middle East.

When WikiLeaks began to publish leaks from US intelligence and military sources, however, the organization became a lightning rod for controversy and the target of US intelligence and national security officials. In one highly publicized case in April 2010, WikiLeaks released a classified video filmed from an Apache helicopter showing the killing of ten Iraqi citizens and two Reuters journalists. Known as the "Collateral Murder" video, it garnered international attention and led to global debate on American actions in the Middle East.

Later in 2010, WikiLeaks began releasing scores of classified US diplomatic cables, which were initially published in five major newspapers: the *New York Times*, Britain's the *Guardian*, Germany's *Der Spiegel*, France's *Le Monde*, and Spain's *El País*. The cables revealed a range of sensitive information. As the WikiLeaks website describes it, they

> show the extent of US spying on its allies and the UN; turning a blind eye to corruption and human rights abuse in "client states"; backroom deals with supposedly neutral countries; lobbying for US corporations; and the measures US diplomats take to advance those who have access to

them. This document release reveals the contradictions between the US's public persona and what it says behind closed doors—and shows that if citizens in a democracy want their governments to reflect their wishes, they should ask to see what's going on behind the scenes.

As the transcripts of the so-called Cablegate documents appeared in newspapers around the world, the US government, especially the State Department, was forced to deal with the far-reaching implications for ongoing diplomatic efforts, political initiatives and partnerships, and US foreign relations. At the very least, many of the revelations exposed diplomatic personnel to embarrassment and discomfort. At the worst, some of the information revealed the secret identities of US intelligence agents and their informants, which put lives at risk and ruined careers; exposed covert US intelligence and diplomatic efforts to foreign governments; and put a chill on intelligence sharing in the US government, further damaging national security. Critics attacked WikiLeaks as a criminal organization bent on aiding terrorists to bring down the United States and called for the US government to shut down the controversial group before it did any more damage.

By late 2010, it seemed as though US lawmakers concurred and were taking action to shut down WikiLeaks. On December 1, 2010, Senator Joe Lieberman announced that Amazon had axed WikiLeaks from its servers. In a statement, he declared that Amazon's "decision to cut off WikiLeaks now is the right decision and should set the standard for other companies WikiLeaks is using to distribute its illegally seized material."

In the next few days, several other companies also cut off WikiLeaks from its servers. One of those companies, Tableau Software, acknowledged that it had acted under pressure from Senator Lieberman. While the other technology companies offered other reasons, many believe that actions taken against

WikiLeaks were in response to pressure from Senator Lieberman and the US Department of Homeland Security.

Although many officials celebrated the actions taken against WikiLeaks, many civil libertarians and free-speech activists were alarmed. It confirmed widespread fears that private companies like Amazon and Tableau held too much power on the Internet and could limit access to information—and even limit access to the Internet itself. The WikiLeaks scandal also showed that governments could successfully pressure companies to censor information and threaten Internet freedom.

The debate over WikiLeaks is one of the topics discussed in the following chapter, which explores the question of whether the Internet should be censored. Other viewpoints included in the chapter consider the role of government regulation in fostering Internet freedom, the efficacy of Internet censorship, and the growing controversy over Internet sovereignty.

"Internet sovereignty' is . . . ultimately about securing the rights and freedoms of its netizens."

Internet Sovereignty— A New Paradigm of Internet Governance

Min Jiang

Min Jiang is associate professor of communication studies at the University of North Carolina–Charlotte and serves as an affiliate researcher at the Center for Global Communication Studies at the University of Pennsylvania. In the following viewpoint, she delineates the conflicting perspectives on Internet control articulated at the 2012 World Conference on International Telecommunications (WCIT-12) in Dubai, United Emirates, December 3-14, 2012: the "Internet freedom" agenda pushed by the United States, Japan, and Europe; and the "Internet sovereignty" model backed by China, Russia, and others. Jiang points out that many regulatory functions and practices carried out by national governments invested in protecting Internet freedom are crucial to maintaining free expression on the Internet and fostering innovation. Several countries, including China, have applied a nar-

row and controlling version of Internet sovereignty to their own Internet-using citizens, or netizens, that has censored much Internet expression and activity. Jiang asserts, prior to the Snowden affair, that the United States and other liberal countries must lead by example and do more to support netizen rights and a more open Internet.

As you read, consider the following questions:

1. According to Jiang, how many countries signed the WCIT-12 treaty?

2. How many countries does the author say did not sign the WCIT-12 treaty?

3. What is China's real-name registration policy, according to Jiang?

"The conference was not about Internet control or Internet governance," said Hamadoun Touré, the head of the Internet Telecommunications Union (ITU), at the closing session of the World Conference on International Telecommunications (WCIT-12) on December 14, 2012 in Dubai. But of course, Mr. Touré was simply denying the obvious. Internet control is precisely what WCIT-12 was about and the ideological divisions between the US-led delegations and the pact headed by China and Russia couldn't have been more visible. While the outcome of WCIT-12 has little substance, China's stance on "Internet sovereignty" warrants our concerns.

The Impact of WCIT-12

Despite the attention and hysteria WCIT-12 has garnered, including provoking an Op-ed from Vint Cerf, the "father of the Internet," calling to keep the Internet open, WCIT-12's actual impact is very minimal, if not entirely negligible. In the end, the Dubai conference, which seeks to affirm nation-state-based regulation of the Internet, produced a non-binding resolution. However, the divisive voting blocs are telling. Of the 144 countries with the right to sign the new treaty, 89 (including China, Russia, and many Arab countries) did so, while 55 (including the U.S., EU [European Union] member states, Japan, and India) said no. Whatever binding resolution WCIT-12 failed to score, the cacophony and what it represents is worth dissecting.

First, the conflict between the US "Internet freedom" agenda and the Sino-Russian vision of "Internet sovereignty" finally played out in the open internationally, dubbed by some as a digital cold war. As I argued in a 2010[1] paper following the conflict between Beijing [China] and Google, China's approach to Internet regulation is based on a highly restrictive notion of "Internet sovereignty" that favors the authority of a nation-state over its netizens. Such an approach stands in direct opposition to the US "Internet freedom" model, the latter at least rhetorically defending the rights of average netizens and the openness of the Internet. WCIT-12 represents an effort by the "yes" voting bloc countries to divert power and responsibilities away from a multi-stakeholder ICANN [Internet Corporation for Assigned Names and Numbers] model to a more state-centered UN model.

The Role of National Governments

Second, it is a mistake to overstate the regulatory power of international institutions traditionally associated with Internet governance (e.g., ICANN or IGF [Internet Governance Forum]). [In their 2012 paper "Where Is the Governance in Internet Governance?" professors Michel J.G.] Van Eeten and [Milton] Mueller argued persuasively that more crucial regulatory functions and practices have in fact been carried out by national governments, Internet service providers (ISPs), and other actors outside the typical "Internet governance" framework over a wide range of issues such as security, copyright infringement, and content regulation. A more holistic view of

---

1. "Authoritarian Informationalism: China's Approach to Internet Sovereignty" by Professor Min Jiang http://papers.ssrn.com/sol3/papers.cfm?abstract_id=1702128.

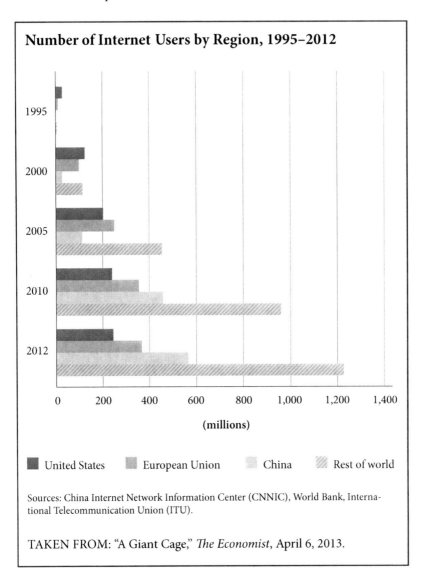

Number of Internet Users by Region, 1995–2012

Sources: China Internet Network Information Center (CNNIC), World Bank, International Telecommunication Union (ITU).

TAKEN FROM: "A Giant Cage," *The Economist*, April 6, 2013.

"Internet governance" should address various aspects of governance issues to include, as [American University professor Laura] DeNardis outlines [in her 2010 working paper "The Emerging Field of Internet Governance,"]: 1) critical Internet resources (e.g., fiber optic cables, routers, IP addresses, and domain names); 2) Internet protocols (e.g., ICT/IP, VoIP, MP3 and other technical standards); 3) online intellectual property rights (Internet-related patents, copyright, trademark); 4) Internet security and infrastructure management (e.g., cyber attack and cyber crime); and 5) communication rights (e.g., freedom of expression, privacy, and reputation).

Third, while it is important to work within international Internet governance bodies that serve as information centers for various member countries and Internet sectors, decisions over a given network primarily resides at the national level, as is the case in China. Over the past 25 years, Beijing not only has built its Web infrastructures, including opening a floodgate of opportunities to private sectors and foreign investors, it has also made sure that such infrastructures remain "Chinese." Besides constructing the well-known Great Firewall, the Chinese central government has ensured that China's national Internet backbone remains firmly in the hands of a few China's national champions such as China Telecom and that application-level ISPs operated mainly by the private sector remain "politically correct" through self-censorship. Overall, the state adopts a multi-layered censorship approach, from blunt suppression of dissidents, Internet policing, content removal, discipline of cyber cafes, to more subtle forms: regulation of ISPs, promotion of self-censorship among users, and employment of cyber commentators to shape public opinion.

Finally, despite the lack of impact WCIT-12 has, the symbolic voting bloc of 89 countries favoring a state-centric model of Internet governance may boost the "legitimacy" of domestic Internet regulations rhetorically, no matter how strenuous and weak the rationale for more regulation. A case in point is China's "real name registration policy" that was first introduced to microblogging services at the end of 2011 and most recently extended nationwide to all ISPs. The law would require China's 564 [618 million by the end of 2013] million Internet users to register their ID information (via national ID card, valid mobile phone number, etc.) with their ISPs before posting comments.

The Future of Internet Sovereignty

As we enter a new Internet world, the Global South will play an increasingly more important role, largely due to their potentially large Internet user base and also their improving economies. On the other hand, the Global South also includes some of the weakest states, conflict zones, and strong authoritarian countries, many of whom look to China. If the WCIT-12 is any indication, the "Internet sovereignty" approach of Internet governance that China favors and advocates holds much sway in the Global South and is likely to persist in the decades to come.

For the U.S. and other liberal countries favoring a more open Internet and netizen rights, much can be done. First and foremost, these countries must lead by example and live up to the promise of "Internet freedom" to shun charges of hypocrisy. For instance, the international reputation of the U.S. has been severely tarnished by the unpopular Iraqi War, American financial crisis and gridlock politics of Washington. "Internet freedom" will fall flat if it fails to defend netizen freedom in practice or foster innovations. Second, avoid SOPA [Stop Online Piracy Act], PIPA [Protect IP Act]-like debacles. More could be done to strengthen civil society groups and chart out a better course between conflicting interests of users and the profit-maximizing tendencies of Internet giants. Last but not least, strike a better balance between liberty and security, transparency and confidentiality, and foster tolerance and civility through community norms and education. After all, "Internet sovereignty" is not about enhancing a particular government's ability and prowess to regulate the Internet but ultimately about securing the rights and freedoms of its netizens.

"We must be wary of [government] agendas and united in our shared conviction that human rights apply online."

Internet Censorship by Governments Is a Human Rights Violation

Hillary Clinton

Hillary Clinton is a former First Lady, US senator, and US secretary of state. In the following viewpoint taken from her remarks opening the 2011 Internet Freedom Conference, she asserts the importance of implementing a global commitment to protect human rights online. Clinton perceives Internet access and freedom to be a human right, and deems it the responsibility of the global community to support human rights and fundamental freedoms worldwide. She challenges the private sector to embrace its role in this struggle and national governments to resist the urge to clamp down and limit Internet freedom. She pushes for a global coalition to protect an open Internet and support cyberactivists and bloggers, several of whom have been oppressed or imprisoned by their own governments for their online publications.

Hillary Clinton, "Remarks at the Conference on Internet Freedom," December 8, 2011, US State Department.

As you read, consider the following questions:

1. According to Clinton, how many people worldwide are Internet users?

2. What country does the author identify as the target of sanctions imposed by the United States and European Union in 2011?

3. According to the Committee to Protect Journalists, as cited by Clinton, what percentage of writers, editors, and photojournalists imprisoned around the world are online journalists?

Now, in two days, on December 10th, [2011,] we'll celebrate Human Rights Day, which is the anniversary of the adoption of the Universal Declaration of Human Rights. And in the 63 years since that achievement, the world has been implementing a global commitment around the rights and freedoms of people everywhere, no matter where they live or who they are. And today, as people increasingly turn to the internet to conduct important aspects of their lives, we have to make sure that human rights are as respected online as offline. After all, the right to express one's views, practice one's faith, peacefully assemble with others to pursue political or social change—these are all rights to which all human beings are entitled, whether they choose to exercise them in a city square or an internet chat room. And just as we have worked together since the last century to secure these rights in the material world, we must work together in this century to secure them in cyberspace.

An Urgent Task

This is an urgent task. It is most urgent, of course, for those around the world whose words are now censored, who are imprisoned because of what they or others have written online, who are blocked from accessing entire categories of internet content, or who are being tracked by governments seeking to keep them from connecting with one another.

In Syria, a blogger named Anas Maarawi was arrested on July 1st after demanding that President [Bashar al-]Asad leave. He's not been charged with anything, but he remains in detention. In both Syria and Iran, many other online activists—actually too many to name—have been detained, imprisoned, beaten, and even killed for expressing their views and organizing their fellow citizens. And perhaps the most well known blogger in Russia, Alexei Navalny, was sentenced on Tuesday to 15 days in jail after he took part in protests over the Russian elections.

In China, several dozen companies signed a pledge in October [2011], committing to strengthen their "self-management, self-restraint, and strict self-discipline." Now, if they were talking about fiscal responsibility, we might all agree. But they were talking about offering web-based services to the Chinese people, which is code for getting in line with the government's tight control over the internet.

Now, these and many other incidents worldwide remind us of the stakes in this struggle. And the struggle does not belong only to those on the front lines and who are suffering. It belongs to all of us: first, because we all have a responsibility to support human rights and fundamental freedoms everywhere. Second, because the benefits of the network grow as the number of users grow. The internet is not exhaustible or competitive. My use of the internet doesn't diminish yours. On the contrary, the more people that are online and contributing ideas, the more valuable the entire network becomes to all the other users. In this way, all users, through the billions of individual choices we make about what information to seek or share, fuel innovation, enliven public debates, quench a thirst for knowledge, and connect people in ways that distance and cost made impossible just a generation ago.

The Importance of Internet Access

But when ideas are blocked, information deleted, conversations stifled, and people constrained in their choices, the internet is diminished for all of us. What we do today to preserve fundamental freedoms online will have a profound effect on the next generation of users. More than two billion people are now connected to the internet, but in the next 20 years, that number will more than double. And we are quickly approaching the day when more than a billion people are using the internet in repressive countries. The pledges we make and the actions we take today can help us determine whether that number grows or shrinks, or whether the meaning of being on the internet is totally distorted.

Delivering on internet freedom requires cooperative actions, and we have to foster a global conversation based on shared principles and with the right partners to navigate the practical challenges of maintaining an internet that is open and free while also interoperable, secure, and reliable. Now, this enterprise isn't a matter of negotiating a single document and calling the job done. It requires an ongoing effort to reckon with the new reality that we live in, in a digital world, and doing so in a way that maximizes its promise.

Challenges and Opportunities

Because the advent of cyberspace creates new challenges and opportunities in terms of security, the digital economy, and human rights, we have to be constantly evolving in our responses. And though they are distinct, they are practically inseparable, because there isn't an economic internet, a social internet, and a political internet. There is just the internet, and we're here to protect what makes it great. . . .

I'd like to briefly discuss three specific challenges that defenders of the internet must confront.

The first challenge is for the private sector to embrace its role in protecting internet freedom, because whether you like it or not, the choices that private companies make have an impact on how information flows or doesn't flow on the internet and mobile networks. They also have an impact on what governments can and can't do, and they have an impact on people on the ground.

In recent months, we've seen cases where companies, products, and services were used as tools of oppression. Now, in some instances, this cannot be foreseen, but in others, yes, it can. A few years ago, the headlines were about companies turning over sensitive information about political dissidents. Earlier this year [2011], they were about a company shutting down the social networking accounts of activists in the midst of a political debate. Today's news stories are about companies selling the hardware and software of repression to authoritarian governments. When companies sell surveillance equipment to the security agency of Syria or Iran or, in past times, [Libyan dictator Muammar] Qadhafi, there can be no doubt it will be used to violate rights.

Economic Sanctions

Now, there are some who would say that in order to compel good behavior by businesses, responsible governments should simply impose broad sanctions, and that will take care of the problem. Well, it's true that sanctions and export controls are useful tools, and the United States makes vigorous use of them when appropriate; and if they are broken, we investigate and pursue violators. And we're always seeking to work with our partners, such as the European Union [EU], to make them as smart and effective as possible. Just last week, for example, we were glad to see our EU partners impose new sanctions on technology going to Syria.

So sanctions are part of the solution, but they are not the entire solution. Dual-use technologies and third-party sales make it impossible to have a sanctions regime that perfectly prevents bad actors from using technologies in bad ways.

Now, sometimes companies say to us at the State Department, "Just tell us what to do, and we'll do it." But the fact is, you can't wait for instructions. In the 21st century, smart companies have to act before they find themselves in the crosshairs of controversy.

I wish there were, but there isn't, an easy formula for this. Making good decisions about how and whether to do business in various parts of the world, particularly where the laws are applied haphazardly or they are opaque, takes critical thinking and deliberation and asking hard questions. So what kind of business should you do in a country where it has a history of violating internet freedom? Is there something you can do to prevent governments from using your products to spy on their own citizens? Should you include warnings to consumers? How will you handle requests for information from security authorities when those requests come without a warrant? Are you working to prevent post-purchase modifications of your products or resale through middlemen to authoritarian regimes?

Developing Responsible Corporate Practices

Now, these and others are difficult questions, but companies must ask them. And the rest of us stand ready to work with you to find answers and to hold those who ignore or dismiss or deny the importance of this issue accountable. A range of resources emerged in recent years to help companies work through these issues. The UN Guiding Principles on Business and Human Rights, which were adopted in June, and the OECD [Organisation for Economic Cooperation and Development] Guidelines for Multinational Enterprises both advise companies on how to meet responsibilities and carry out due diligence. And the Global Network Initiative, which is represented here tonight, is a growing forum where companies can work through challenges with other industry partners, as well as academics, investors, and activists.

And of course, companies can always learn from users. The Silicon Valley Human Rights Conference in October brought together companies, activists, and experts to discuss real life problems and identify solutions. And some participants issued what they called the Silicon Valley Standard for stakeholders to aspire to.

Working through these difficult questions by corporate executives and board members should help shape your practices. Part of the job of responsible corporate management in the 21st century is doing human rights due diligence on new markets, instituting internal review procedures, identifying principles by which decisions are to be made in tough situations, because we cannot let the short-term gains that all of us think are legitimate and worth seeking jeopardize the openness of the internet and human rights of individuals who use it without it coming back to haunt us all in the future. Because a free and open internet is important not just to technology companies but to all companies. Whether it's run with a single mobile phone or an extensive corporate network, it's hard to find any business today that doesn't depend in some way on the internet and doesn't suffer when networks are constrained.

And also I would add that, in this day, brand and reputation are precious corporate assets. Companies that put them at risk when they are careless about freedom of the internet can often pay a price.

So I think it's particularly appropriate and important that the private sector is strongly represented at this meeting and that Google is co-hosting tonight's event. In both securing the promise of a free and open internet and managing the risks that new technologies raise, the private sector is a crucial partner.

The Role of Government

But even as companies must step up, governments must resist the urge to clamp down, and that is the second challenge we face. If we're not careful, governments could upend the current internet governance framework in a quest to increase their own control. Some governments use internet governance issues as a cover for pushing an agenda that would justify restricting human rights online. We must be wary of such agendas and united in our shared conviction that human rights apply online.

So right now, in various international forums, some countries are working to change how the internet is governed. They want to replace the current multi-stakeholder approach, which includes governments, the private sector, and citizens, and supports the free flow of information, in a single global network. In its place, they aim to impose a system cemented in a global code that expands control over internet resources, institutions, and content, and centralizes that control in the hands of governments.

Now, in a way, that isn't surprising, because governments have never met a voice or public sphere they didn't want to control at some point or another. They want to control what gets printed in newspapers, who gets into universities, what companies get oil contracts, what churches and NGOs [nongovernmental organizations] get registered, where citizens can gather, so why not the internet? But it's actually worse than that. It's not just that they want governments to have all the control by cutting out civil society and the private sector; they also want to empower each individual government to make their own rules for the internet that not only undermine human rights and the free flow of information but also the interoperability of the network.

In effect, the governments pushing this agenda want to create national barriers in cyberspace. This approach would be disastrous for internet freedom. More government control will further constrict what people in repressive environments can do online. It would also be disastrous for the internet as a whole, because it would reduce the dynamism of the internet for everyone. Fragmenting the global internet by erecting barriers around national internets would change the landscape of cyberspace. In this scenario, the internet would contain people in a series of digital bubbles, rather than connecting them in a global network. Breaking the internet into pieces would give you echo chambers rather than an innovative global marketplace of ideas.

The US Position on Internet Freedom

The United States wants the internet to remain a space where economic, political, and social exchanges flourish. To do that, we need to protect people who exercise their rights online, and we also need to protect the internet itself from plans that would undermine its fundamental characteristics.

Now, those who push these plans often do so in the name of security. And let me be clear: The challenge of maintaining security and of combating cyber crime, such as the theft of intellectual property, are real—a point I underscore whenever I discuss these issues. There are predators, terrorists, traffickers on the internet, malign actors plotting cyber attacks, and they all need to be stopped. We can do that by working together without compromising the global network, its dynamism, or our principles.

Now, there's a lot to be said about cyber security. I won't go into that tonight. I'll be talking about it more, but my basic point is that the United States supports the public-private collaboration that now exists to manage the technical evolution of the internet in real time. We support the principles of multi-stakeholder internet governance developed by more than 30 nations in the OECD earlier this year. A multi-stakeholder system brings together the best of governments, the private sector, and civil society. And most importantly, it works. It has kept the internet up and running for years all over the world. So to use an American phrase, our position is,

"If it ain't broke, don't fix it." And there's no good reason to replace an effective system with an oppressive one.

A Global Coalition

The third and final challenge is that all of us—governments, private sector, civil society—must do more to build a truly global coalition to preserve an open internet. And that's where all of you here today come in, because internet freedom cannot be defended by one country or one region alone. Building this global coalition is hard, partly because for people in many countries the potential of the internet is still unrealized. While it's easy for us in the United States or in the Netherlands to imagine what we would lose if the internet became less free, it is harder for those who have yet to see the benefit of the internet in their day to day lives. So we have to work harder to make the case that an open internet is and will be in everyone's best interests. And we have to keep that in mind as we work to build this global coalition and make the case to leaders of those countries where the next generation of internet users live. These leaders have an opportunity today to help ensure that the full benefits are available to their people tomorrow, and in so doing, they will help us ensure an open internet for everyone.

So the United States will be making the case for an open internet in our work worldwide, and we welcome other countries to join us. As our coalition expands, countries like Ghana and Kenya, represented here tonight, Mongolia, Chile, also represented, I saw, Indonesia and others are sure to be effective at bringing other potential partners on board who have perspectives that can help us confront and answer difficult questions. And new players from governments, the private sector, and civil society will be participating in managing the internet in coming decades as billions more people from all different regions go online.

So let's lay the groundwork now for these partnerships that will support an open internet in the future. And in that spirit, I want to call attention to two important items on your agenda for tomorrow. The first will be to build support for a new cross-regional group that will work together in exactly the way that I've just discussed, based on shared principles, providing a platform for governments to engage creatively and energetically with the private sector, civil society, and other governments.

Several countries have already signaled their intention to join. I hope others here will do the same, and going forward, others will endorse the declaration that our Dutch hosts have prepared. . . .

Protecting Activists and Bloggers

The second item I want to highlight is a practical effort to do more to support cyber activists and bloggers who are threatened by their repressive governments. The Committee to Protect Journalists recently reported that of all the writers, editors, and photojournalists now imprisoned around the world, nearly half are online journalists. The threat is very real. Now, several of us already provide support, including financial support, to activists and bloggers, and I was pleased that the EU recently announced new funding for that purpose. And I know that other governments, including the Netherlands, are also looking for ways to help out.

By coordinating our efforts, we can make them go further and help more people. Earlier, I heard what the foreign minister here is proposing. And we have talked about creating a digital defenders partnership to be part of this global effort. We hope tomorrow's meetings will give us a chance to discuss with other potential partners how such a partnership could work.

So while we meet here in the Netherlands in this beautiful city to talk about how to keep the internet open, unfortunately some countries are pulling very hard in the opposite direction. They're trying to erect walls between different activities online, economic exchanges, political discussions, religious expression, social interaction, and so on. They want to keep what they like and which doesn't threaten them and suppress what they don't. But there are opportunity costs for trying to be open for business but closed for free expression, costs to a nation's education system, political stability, social mobility, and economic potential.

And walls that divide the internet are easier to erect than to maintain. Our government will continue to work very hard to get around every barrier that repressive governments put up, because governments that have erected barriers will eventually find themselves boxed in, and they will face the dictator's dilemma. They will have to choose between letting the walls fall or paying the price for keeping them standing by resorting to greater repression and to escalating the opportunity cost of missing out on the ideas that have been blocked and the people who have disappeared.

I urge countries everywhere, instead of that alternative dark vision, join us here today in the bet that we are making, a bet that an open internet will lead to stronger, more prosperous countries. This is not a bet on computers or mobile phones. It's a bet on the human spirit. It's a bet on people. And we're confident that together, with our partners and government, the private sector, and civil society around the world, who have made this same bet like all of you here tonight, we will preserve the internet as open and secure for all.

On the eve of Human Rights Day, this meeting reminds us of the timeless principles that should be our north star. And a look at the world around us and the way it is changing reminds us there is no auto-pilot steering us forward. We have to work in good faith and engage in honest debate, and we have to join together to solve the challenges and seize the opportunities of this exciting digital age. Thank you all for being committed to that goal and that vision. The United States pledges our support and our partnership going forward.

"This debate between Internet freedom
and sovereignty is an oversimplification
and ultimately a false choice."

There Is Middle Ground Between Internet Freedom and Internet Sovereignty

Scott J. Shackelford

Scott J. Shackelford is an author, educator, and fellow at the Center for Applied Cybersecurity Research. In the following viewpoint, he contends that the growing concern over the apparently opposing approaches to the Internet at the 2012 World Conference on International Telecommunications (WCIT) is overblown. Shackelford rejects the depiction of the conference as a battle between the forces of Internet freedom and the forces of Internet censorship, maintaining that the situation is much more complicated. Instead of focusing on the differences highlighted by WCIT, Shackelford argues, it would be more productive to con-

Scott J. Shackelford, "The Coming Age of Internet Sovereignty?," *Huffington Post*, January 10, 2013. Excerpts of this essay have been published in various outlets, including: Scott J. Shackelford, *Managing Cyber Attacks in International Law, Business and Relations: In Search of Cyber Peace* (Cambridge University Press, 2014); Scott J. Shackelford, "Toward Cyber Peace: Managing Cyber Attacks Through Polycentric Governance," 62 *American University Law Review* 1273 (2013); Scott J. Shackelford and Amanda N. Craig, "Beyond the New 'Digital Divide': Analyzing the Evolving Role of Governments in Internet Governance and Enhancing Cybersecurity," *Stanford Journal of International Law* (2014). Copyright © 2013 by Scott J. Shackelford. All rights reserved. Reproduced by permission.

centrate on areas in which countries can find common ground. The United States and other countries that support Internet freedom should view the outcome of WCIT as a call to action and to practice Internet freedom, he says, providing a model for other nations around the world.

As you read, consider the following questions:

1. According to Shackelford, what year were the International Telecommunication Regulations (ITRs) written?

2. According to the June 2012 Global Transparency Report cited by Shackelford, how many requests did Google receive between July and December 2011 to remove content or provide information about its users from governments around the world?

3. How many countries does the author say routinely monitor Internet traffic?

In few places on Earth is censorship undertaken more vigorously than it is in the People's Republic of China (PRC). Take Amazon.com. At one level, Amazon.cn, allegedly the world's largest Chinese online bookstore, resembles its American counterpart, selling everything from the *Twilight series* to *Battlestar Galactica*. But dig deeper, and differences multiply. A search in early 2011 revealed only a single hit for "human rights in China": Alexandra Harney's *The China Price*. Perhaps most telling was a query conducted by the *New York Times* in 2010 for "censorship" and "China," that returned a result for a book entitled, *When China Rules the World*.

What does such censorship mean for the rest of the world's Internet users? If the worst predictions of the recently concluded World Conference on International Telecommunications (WCIT) are correct, the Internet experience in more countries could resemble that of China, threatening the dawn of a new age of Internet sovereignty. But such dire warnings may be simplistic and overblown.

History of the ITU

ITU was founded in Paris in 1865 as the International Telegraph Union. It took its present name in 1932, and in 1947 became a specialized agency of the United Nations. Although its first area of expertise was the telegraph, the work of ITU now covers the whole ICT [information and communications technology] sector, from digital broadcasting to the Internet, and from mobile technologies to 3D TV. An organization of public-private partnership since its inception, ITU currently has a membership of 193 countries and some 700 private-sector entities. ITU is headquartered in Geneva, Switzerland, and has twelve regional and area offices around the world.

International Telecommunication Union,
"History," 2013. www.itu.int.

The WCIT was held under the auspices of the International Telecommunication Union (ITU), which is a UN body responsible for managing its namesake—information and telecommunication technologies. In recent years, the ITU has moved towards the center of a debate about how the Internet should be managed, offering an institutional alternative to the collection of private sector actors, such as ICANN [Internet Corporation for Assigned Names and Numbers], that largely manage the Internet today. Ahead of the WCIT, the secretary general of the ITU, Hamadoun Touré, assured stakeholders that the ITU was not interested in making a power grab for Internet governance. But things turned out differently.

Growing Concerns at the WCIT

During the WCIT, 193 countries worked to revise the International Telecommunication Regulations (ITRs), which were written in 1988 to "define the general principles for the provision and operation of international telecommunications." Vinton Cerf, the "Father of the Internet," told Congress that new ITRs could undermine the Internet's openness and "lead to 'top-down control dictated by government.'" Numerous U.S. congressional representatives expressed similar sentiments.

To some degree, these concerns seem to have been borne out. Eighty-nine countries signed the WCIT final resolution that on the one hand embraces multistakeholder governance, but on the other determines that "all governments should have an equal role and responsibility for international Internet governance and for ensuring the stability, security and continuity of the existing Internet." This language seems to herald a growing state-centric view of cyberspace held by many nations, especially in Asia (with the notable exceptions of India, Japan, and Australia) and Africa. Such a view could lead to more regulations on content—what we generally think of as censorship—among other restrictions. Indeed, there is a key distinction between how the United States and other countries, such as China, claim to view cyberspace—but the situation is not as black and white as it may first appear.

The True State of Internet Freedom

The United States has a stated policy of promoting a single global networked commons where freedom of speech is sacrosanct—even as the White House has sought the ability to monitor that speech through stepped-up wiretapping. Indeed, the [Barack] Obama administration has promoted Internet freedom abroad, but content is not insulated at home. For example, Google publishes information about governments that have requested information about its users or asked it to remove content. According to a June 2012 Global Transparency Report, between July and December 2011, Google received 1,000 such requests and complied with over half of them. These included Western democracies like Spain, Poland, and the United States, the latter of which reportedly submitted more requests than any other country.

China, on the other hand, along with many other nations, is viewed as building digital barriers in the name of Internet sovereignty. Consider the case of Iran, which reportedly is building a national network detached from the global Internet to enhance governmental control of information and, potentially, better guard against cyber attacks. And while Iran's efforts are more extreme than many nations', it is not alone. Ethiopia, Cuba, and more than 40 other nations now routinely monitor Internet traffic. These nations are part of a growing club that seems to balk at the notion of Internet freedom.

But this debate between Internet freedom and sovereignty is an oversimplification and ultimately a false choice. Instead of a black and white comparison, what may be more accurate is investigating the 50 (or potentially 193) shades of gray that comprise the complexion of global Internet regulations to find common ground. Even if we are not heading for an age of outright Internet balkanization, we may be in for a period of greater state involvement in Internet governance. The open questions are: what costs will this impose in terms of innovation and interconnectedness, and how can we manage the growing reach of the leviathan to minimize distortions and protect civil liberties?

Finding Opportunities

The United States contributes to this debate by trumpeting Internet freedom and the benefits of a more decentralized approach to Internet governance. These calls were not heeded at the WCIT, but that does not mean that it is time to disband the ITU. At most, the non-binding WCIT resolution helps provide legal cover for countries that are already taking a heavier hand in Internet governance. This trend would not stop with the demise of the ITU. Yet it is also true that the fact that the ITU is a state-centric UN organization with a circumscribed role for the private sector that militates against expanding its scope.

An opportunity to instill the Internet freedom agenda may have been missed at the WCIT, but that does not mean that the Internet as we know it is over. Instead, it should be taken as a call to action for Western nations, including the United States, to practice what we preach, and to work with our partners around the world to build consensus on the future of Internet governance in an increasingly multipolar world.

| "The very existence of WikiLeaks is a
threat to national security."

WikiLeaks Is a National Security Threat and Should Be Censored

Marc Thiessen

Marc Thiessen is a visiting fellow with the American Enterprise Institute and writes a weekly column for the Washington Post. *In the following viewpoint, he identifies WikiLeaks as a serious national security threat to the United States. Thiessen maintains that WikiLeaks and its founder, Julian Assange, are determined to harm the United States by releasing classified documents online, which endangers American allies and operatives and reveals clandestine operations and secret communications. He criticizes the tepid US response to the WikiLeaks disclosures, arguing that the Barack Obama administration should act more forcefully to shut down WikiLeaks before it does further damage to US diplomatic and military efforts overseas.*

As you read, consider the following questions:

1. According to Thiessen, how many stolen classified documents did WikiLeaks release online in August 2010?

2. How many classified documents regarding the Iraq War did WikiLeaks release online in October 2010, according to the author?

3. How many websites does Thiessen claim were shut down by the US government for disseminating pirated music and movies?

Is the United States of America really powerless to stop a nomadic cyber-hacker—who sleeps on people's couches and changes his hair color to avoid surveillance—from causing enormous damage to our national security?

Apparently, in the age of [President Barack] Obama, we are.

The Threat of WikiLeaks

Four months ago [in August 2010], the criminal enterprise WikiLeaks released more than 75,000 stolen classified documents that, among other things, revealed the identities of more than 100 Afghans who were cooperating with America against the Taliban. The Obama administration condemned WikiLeaks' actions. The Justice Department said it was weighing criminal charges against WikiLeaks founder Julian Assange. The Pentagon warned that if WikiLeaks did not stand down and return other stolen documents it possessed, the government would "make them do the right thing."

And then nothing happened.

Last month [October 2010], WikiLeaks struck again—this time posting more than 390,000 classified documents on the war in Iraq. Adm. Mike Mullen, the chairman of the Joint Chiefs of Staff, responded with a Twitter post: "Another irresponsible posting of stolen classified documents by WikiLeaks puts lives at risk and gives adversaries valuable information." Mullen was right—but, with all respect to the chairman, a tweet was not exactly the cyber-response the WikiLeaks disclosures warranted.

The Third Leak

Now, WikiLeaks has struck a third time with what may prove to be its most damaging disclosures yet—a cache of more than 251,287 American diplomatic cables and directives, including more than 117,000 that are classified. According to the *New York Times*, which was given advance copies of the documents, many cables "name diplomats' confidential sources, from foreign legislators and military officers to human rights activists and journalists, often with a warning to Washington: 'Please protect' or 'Strictly protect.'" Other documents detail confidential conversations with foreign leaders, including Arab leaders urging the U.S. to attack Iran's nuclear facilities. Still others could hamper U.S. counterterrorism efforts—such as a cable in which Yemeni leaders say they lied to their own parliament by claiming that Yemeni forces, not Americans, had carried out missile attacks against al-Qaeda. If Yemen responds to this revelation by restricting U.S. efforts to hunt down al-Qaeda, the results could be devastating.

What action did the Obama administration take to prevent the impending release of such volatile information? State Department legal adviser Harold Koh sent a strongly worded letter urging WikiLeaks to cease publishing classified materials. I'm sure that made Assange think twice.

A Tepid Response

Is the Obama administration going to do anything—anything at all—to stop these serial disclosures of our nation's most closely guarded secrets? Just this past week, the federal government took decisive action to shut down more than 70 Web sites that were disseminating pirated music and movies. Hollywood is safe, but WikiLeaks is free to disseminate classified documents without consequence.

With this latest release, Assange may now have illegally disclosed more classified information than anyone in American history. He is in likely violation of the Espionage Act and arguably is providing material support for terrorism. But unlike leakers who came before him, Assange has done more than release information; he has created a virtual system for the ongoing collection and dissemination of America's secrets. The very existence of WikiLeaks is a threat to national security. Unless something is done, WikiLeaks will only grow more brazen—and our unwillingness to stop it will embolden others to reveal classified information using the unlawful medium Assange has built.

WikiLeaks' first disclosures caught the Obama administration by surprise. But how does the administration explain its inaction in the face of WikiLeaks' two subsequent, and increasingly dangerous, releases? In both cases, it had fair warning: Assange announced what kinds of documents he possessed, and he made clear his intention to release them.

Mounting Damage

The Obama administration has the ability to bring Assange to justice and to put WikiLeaks out of business. The new U.S. Cyber Command could shut down WilkiLeaks' servers and prevent them from releasing more classified information on President Obama's orders. But, as [*The Washington Post*] reported this month, the Obama administration has been paralyzed by infighting over how, and when, it might use these new offensive capabilities in cyberspace. One objection: "The State Department is concerned about diplomatic backlash" from any offensive actions in cyberspace, the *Post* reported. Well, now the State Department can deal with the "diplomatic backlash" that comes from standing by helplessly, while WikiLeaks releases hundreds of thousands of its most sensitive diplomatic cables.

Because of its failure to act, responsibility for the damage done by these most recent disclosures now rests with the Obama administration. Perhaps this latest release crosses a line that will finally spur the administration to action. After all, the previous disclosures harmed only our war efforts. But this latest disclosure is a blow to a cause Democrats really care about—our diplomatic efforts. Maybe now, finally, the gloves will come off. Or is posting mournful tweets about the damage done to our national security the best this administration can do?

"The forces that be, led by US Democratic Senator Joe Lieberman, are on a quest to limit our access [to WikiLeaks material]."

The US Government Should Not Pressure Companies to Censor WikiLeaks

Jillian York

Jillian York is a journalist, political activist, and the director of the International Freedom of Expression at the Electronic Frontier Foundation. In the following viewpoint, she describes US efforts to pressure private companies to shut down access to WikiLeaks after it released classified US documents online in 2010. York maintains that such efforts are problematic because they force private companies to interpret and enforce laws and often violate free speech. Much of the material in question, York points out, is not a threat to national security. Private business, Yorks argues, has the obligation to do a better job standing up to government and public pressures to censor Internet speech. Customers must make their voices clear and demand that private companies formulate better policies on free speech issues, York concludes.

As you read, consider the following questions:

1. What US senator does York identify as the leader of the movement toward limiting access to WikiLeaks online?

2. According to the author, how many requests were made by the US government to remove content from Google during a six-month period in 2010?

3. What country does York say that the Internet company LinkedIn blocked access to before it reversed its decision?

WikiLeaks' latest release is making its rounds in the media. Links to cablegate.wikileaks.org are circulating, posted on Twitter and Facebook, passed around in emails. After several releases from the whistleblowing organisation, we've begun to take for granted that the leaked information—at least what's already online—will be accessible to us.

And yet, the forces that be, led by US Democratic Senator Joe Lieberman, are on a quest to limit our access. Earlier this week [early December 2010], after a call from Lieberman, Amazon—which had been hosting the site—booted WikiLeaks from its hosting service. Yesterday a small American company called Tableau took down visualisations based on WikiLeaks data, and Lieberman added WikiLeaks' new host, Swedish company Bahnhof, to his hit list. Early this morning [December 3, 2010], hosting provider Everydns dropped Wikleaks, claiming it had to protect its other clients from attack. Wikileaks has subsequently relocated to a Swiss host.

As [journalist] Rebecca MacKinnon points out, this isn't the first time Lieberman has made such a call; in 2008, the Senator demanded removal of "content produced by Islamist terrorist organisations" from video-sharing site YouTube. The company refused to remove most content, its lawyer noting that it was covered by the First Amendment.

What Is WikiLeaks?

WikiLeaks is a nonprofit organization based in Sweden that makes sensitive and classified information available to the public via its website, wikileaks.org. The administrators of the site focus on documents that expose actions they view as criminal or unethical, particularly actions committed by governments or corporations. The material available on WikiLeaks is donated by anonymous individuals. WikiLeaks takes great pains to ensure that those who leak the documents remain anonymous for their own protection, and these donors are often unknown even to the administrators of the site. Within five years of its launch in 2006, WikiLeaks became recognized as one of the world's leading sources of leaked information and changed the way that many people view modern investigative journalism.

"*WikiLeaks,*" Global Issues in Context Online Collection, *2013.*

A Troubling Trend

There is, of course, a precedent for content removal at government request as well—plenty of it, in fact. Earlier this year, Google made public government requests for data, as well as for content removal—in the United States, the latter came in at 128 for a six month-period. During the same period, the UK made 48 such requests.

These examples represent a broader trend, which [blogger and Internet activist] Ethan Zuckerman has termed "intermediary censorship." It isn't always about national security, nor is it always at the behest of a government, but increasingly, American companies are removing protected speech from their servers.

Of course, these private companies have every right to set their own rules, by which users are expected to abide. Despite the calls from Lieberman, Amazon claims their terms of service were violated by WikiLeaks posting content to which they didn't own the rights. Observers shouldn't be too surprised: in another recent case, Amazon removed a book on paedophilia in response to public pressure. Webhost Rackspace removed the website of controversial Quran-burning pastor Terry Jones. And social networking sites like Facebook and YouTube regularly remove content that violate their terms of service.

Sometimes those removals are a result of attempts, however misguided, to abide by the law. In 2009, American webhost Bluehost cut off service from a Zimbabwean activist group in an attempt to abide by US export control laws; as it turned out, the hosting company was being overly cautious and reversed its decision. In a similar incident, LinkedIn blocked access to the entire country of Syria, a decision that was also reversed when the company learned they had over-complied.

Protecting Free Speech

Again, all of these companies were well within their *rights*—the question is, do they have a responsibility to uphold the principles of free speech? Should the role they play as part of the public sphere have an effect on how they police their customers?

Citizens around the world are increasingly dependent on privately-owned spaces for carrying public discourse. We read our news, engage in political debate, write blog posts. But the more dependent we become on online platforms to exercise our right to free speech, the worse we'll feel it when the rug is swept out from under us.

Amazon's confirmation that they removed WikiLeaks because of a terms of service violation—and not because of a government request—should alarm us all. Once companies start deciding for themselves who has violated the law, they are effectively taking that law into their own hands.

The Future of Internet Speech

The fact of the matter is, it is neither cost-effective nor easy to host one's own content, and so most of us are now bound to the rules and regulations of companies. As Rebecca MacKinnon writes: "The future of freedom in the Internet age may well depend on whether we the people can succeed in holding companies that now act as arbiters of the public discourse accountable to the public interest."

If we want to uphold our right to free expression, the answer is clear: As the customers, we must make our voices heard to the companies that control our content. This means supporting initiatives that push for companies to create better policies for content regulation. This also means speaking loudly with our money, and taking our business to companies that respect the principles of free expression.

Periodical and Internet Sources Bibliography

The following articles have been selected to supplement the diverse views presented in this chapter.

Nathaniel Borenstein	"Vint Cerf Is Too Modest; Internet Access Is a Human Right," *Huffington Post*, December 1, 2012. www.huffingtonpost.com.
Mary Kate Cary	"The Real WikiLeaks Threat," *U.S. News & World Report*, December 9, 2010.
Vinton G. Cerf	"Internet Access Is Not a Human Right," *New York Times*, January 4, 2012.
Chris Coons	"Internet Freedom Is a Human Right," *Huffington Post*, May 10, 2012. www.huffingtonpost .com.
Rogier Creemers	"The Internet, Soft War, Sovereignty, and China," *World Policy Blog*, July 11, 2012. www .worldpolicy.org.
The Economist	"China's Internet: A Giant Cage," April 6, 2013.
Adam Clark Estes	"The Case for (and Against) Internet as a Human Right," *Atlantic Wire*, January 5, 2012. www.thewire.com.
Max Fisher	"When Is Government Web Censorship Justified? An Indian Horror Story," *Atlantic Monthly*, August 22, 2012.
Michael Geist	"Is Internet Connectivity a Human Right?," *Toronto Star*, June 20, 2011.
Rupert Myers	"Internet Access Is Not a 'Human Right'—for Perverts or Anyone Else," *Daily Telegraph* (London), November 13, 2012.

OPPOSING
VIEWPOINTS®
SERIES

CHAPTER 2

Who Should Govern the Internet?

Chapter Preface

The debate over Internet governance came to a head at the World Conference on International Telecommunications (WCIT-12) in Dubai, United Emirates, in early December 2012. The conference brought together 144 delegates from countries all over the world to discuss ways to foster collaboration and innovation in international telecommunication. Two of the key topics were the growth of the Internet and the creation of an atmosphere that would allow it to continue working efficiently and smoothly. Key to this mission would be a coordinated effort to revise the International Telecommunications Regulations (ITRs), a 1988 international treaty negotiated to facilitate the "global interconnection and interoperability" of telecommunications traffic across national borders to better serve the changing telecommunications landscape. According to critics, however, the most significant thing to result from the WCIT-12 conference was a growing controversy over the future of the Internet and who would govern it.

Internet governance has not always been such a hot-button issue. For decades, maintaining the Internet has been left to a multistakeholder model in which technical and policy bodies all play key roles in managing the Internet. In this model, power is decentralized, residing among three main governing groups, which include the International Corporation for Assigned Names and Numbers (ICANN), a private body that coordinates technical aspects of the Internet's underlying address book, the Domain Name System (DNS); the Internet Engineering Task Force (IETF), an open community of researchers, network designers, engineers, and vendors who develop and maintain Internet standards; and the Internet Governance Forum (IGF), a forum for Internet stakeholders to address risks and problems, debate matters of censorship and governance, and find ways to maximize Internet opportunities.

In recent years, however, many observers have noticed a growing displeasure with the multistakeholder model from a number of countries—all of whom want to have more control over the Internet within their borders. Some have already implemented such controls; for example, Chinese authorities censor websites that discuss politically sensitive issues such as the country's human rights record, block access to popular social media sites such as Facebook and Twitter, and closely monitor online conversations, blogs, and forums for potentially subversive material. Many other countries in eastern Europe, Asia, Africa, and the Middle East have also implemented similar Internet censorship and surveillance methods.

The WCIT-12 provided an opportunity for these countries to revisit the issue of Internet governance and find a way to assume greater control. Delegates from these countries began to lobby for the International Telecommunication Union (ITU), an agency of the United Nations, to be empowered to have more regulatory power over the Internet. These delegates asserted that the main stakeholders involved in Internet governance were based in the United States and reflected US concerns and policies. An international body, like the ITU, would do a better job in responding to the Internet needs and concerns of developing countries.

Critics of empowering the ITU for such purposes perceived the proposal to be a power grab—the first steps in shifting power from the decentralized, multistakeholder model currently in place to establishing governmental and intergovernmental control over the Internet. Such a fundamental change in the way the Internet is governed would have dire consequences, critics warn: innovation and commerce would be stifled, democracy suppressed, and human rights trampled. One of the Internet's pioneers, often called the Father of the Internet, Vinton Cerf, declared that any attempt to move away from the multistakeholder model of Internet governance had "the potential to put government handcuffs on the Net. To prevent that—and keep the Internet open and free for the next generations—we need to prevent a fundamental shift in how the Internet is governed."

The WCIT-12 produced no consensus and revealed a deep divide between the two factions. The revised ITRs, which would take a step toward imbuing the ITU with more regulatory power, was signed by eighty-nine countries. The signatories included Russia, China, Brazil, Iran, and Indonesia. Fifty-five countries did not sign the treaty revision, including the United States, Australia, Canada, and the United Kingdom.

The role of the ITU in Internet governance is one of the topics examined in the following chapter, which debates the issue of how the Internet should be governed.

> *"The [International Telecommunication Union] is focused on reaching out to voting member states . . . in order to facilitate an honest, fair-play approach to international telecommunications regulation."*

The United Nations Should Play a Greater Role in Internet Governance

Jean-Christophe Nothias

Jean-Christophe Nothias is the editor in chief of the Global Journal. *In the following viewpoint, he counters the prevalent view of the Internet governance debate as laid out at the 2012 World Conference on International Telecommunications (WCIT-12) in Dubai, United Emirates. Nothias argues that the International Telecommunication Union (ITU), branch of the United Nations, is not launching a power grab for control of the Internet; in fact, he argues, it is the United States that has too much power over Internet policy and regulation, putting developing countries at a disadvantage. He deems the forces lined up to defeat any new initiative or policy proposal at the WCIT-12 as be-*

lievers in the fairy tale of a democratic and fair Internet, but the Internet is already tilted toward powerful nations and private corporations. One seminal figure, Internet pioneer Jon Postel, saw the disparity and turned to the ITU to address it. Instead of relying on "the Internet community"—which is by its nature not democratic and is driven by its own agendas—people need to recognize the hypocrisy of such forces and give consideration to other proposals regarding Internet governance discussed at WCIT-12.

As you read, consider the following questions:

1. According to Nothias, representatives from how many countries are meeting at the WCIT-12 in Dubai?

2. What private corporation located in California does the author say essentially manages and regulates much of the Internet?

3. What percentage of global digital revenues go to Google and Facebook, according to Nothias?

The upcoming World Conference on International Tele-communications (WCIT-12) in Dubai looms as a moment of truth for the Internet's governing rules and economic model. In all, representatives of 193 countries will come together to review the *International Telecommunication Regulations (ITR)* agreed in Melbourne 25 years ago [in 1988].

The United States (US) government, a leading voice in the sector, is strongly opposed to any changes to the treaty (itself an update of an earlier agreement), arguing the Internet has nothing to do with 'traditional' telecommunications, and—more ominously—that freedom is at stake. In contrast to this 'no changes proposed' plan, other member states are likely to bring different perspectives and ideas to feed into discussions at the 11-day December event, which will be moderated by the International Telecommunication Union (ITU), a specialized United Nations (UN) agency. The fight is growing increasingly vocal, while raising questions of concern to all about the overwhelming power of the US in relation to the Internet and the need for structural re-balancing.

A Survey of the Battlefield

Before looking at the critical proposals to be discussed in Dubai, as well as the arguments now flooding the public sphere, however, let's first survey the battlefield where this war is raging.

The ITU Secretariat itself has no power to propose amendments to the *ITR*, nor has the organization expressed a desire to control the Internet. The ITU, as an institution, has the power to adopt amendments, on the basis of consensus of the membership. As a UN body, the ITU's DNA is rooted in notions of human rights and human development, alongside a technical cooperation mandate. None of this would allow room for a power grab. In fact, the ITU is focused on reaching out to voting member states, as well as other concerned players, in order to facilitate an honest, fair-play approach to international telecommunications regulation.

All member states have had the right to circulate proposals to be discussed in Dubai. Each has also been encouraged to launch national consultation processes prior to WCIT-12. The ITU itself has shared preparatory documents online, and initiated a public forum to collect comments and proposals from any interested party. The agency represents a large and open coordinating point where not only governments, but also over 500 private sector entities, members of academia and civil society have been preparing the debate to come. It is noticeable, however, that the most influential non-government player— Google—has never sought to become a consulting member, and in fact has declined several invitations from the ITU Secretariat to do so. At this stage, nobody is able to say with any

65

certainty which proposals, often dramatically opposed, will be adopted at the conference, with any treaty amendments requiring a simple majority.

The Issues

Five key issues form the focus of international wrangling ahead of WCIT-12: net neutrality, payment principles for senders and receivers, control, cyber security and censorship, even though the last three are not on the agenda. Despite the headline-grabbing implications of the latter, however, it is the first two that shape up as perhaps the most critical to the future of the Internet as we know it.

At the most basic level, 'net neutrality' refers to non-discrimination in transiting data packets. The Internet today is going through critical transformations that threaten to create, if left unaddressed, issues of even greater magnitude. For years, data delivery was based on a 'best effort' principle— every connected network operator would do their best to transfer data, with no timing guarantee, defined hierarchy, nor specific quality requirement. Two major challenges, however, are now transforming the industry.

In the context of data, speed is money: all web-based businesses are well aware that speed improves end-user experience, and boosts revenues. On top of constant increases in traffic, video streaming has also emerged as a significant bandwidth consumer. Fierce competition is pushing the market to secure 'quality of service' guarantees around resolution, smooth play and start-up time. A portion of the data circulating today over the Internet will increasingly be subject to contractual commitments, and will need, therefore, to secure top-priority *laissez-passer*. Step by step, the speed issue is creating a split between 'economy class' data, and 'premium' and 'first class' data. Those with the money to pay will be able to afford the best speed and quality. For others, it will be a case of 'we'll take care of you when we have the available bandwidth.'

Equality of Service on the Internet

Arbitrage over which data goes first is an issue impacting all Internet users worldwide. Previously, this was not the case (and no one could complain) due to the 'best-effort' approach. It is clear to many of the Internet industry's major players dealing with Content Delivery Networks (CDNs), Front End Optimization, a new protocol challenging the 30-year-old Transmission Control Protocol and other emerging technologies, that the next competitive battleground is quality, and therefore the need for *reserved* bandwidth.

This will dramatically change the use of the Internet, as well as the revenue share between players. Another significant element of the 'speed battle' relates not to data flows, but to infrastructure capacities. We know that emerging and developing economies are already slow on their own infrastructure development, and facing challenging conditions to identify additional funds to build necessary facilities and purchase equipment to increase broadband access. A parallel infrastructure divide between broadband and non-broadband countries will exacerbate the split in data 'classes.' Similarly, revenues will inevitably follow technology—more to the rich, less to the poor.

WCIT-12 Proposals

Many proposals are on the table ahead of WCIT-12, and it would be meaningless to look into each, as only a few have a chance to achieve a voting majority. One idea by ETNO, the 50-member European Telecommunications Network Operators' Association driving broadband growth in Europe, however, has gained some support and visibility from the ITU membership. African and Arab states have made proposals equivalent in intent, albeit using different language. ETNO's idea concerns Article 3 of the Melbourne treaty:

> Operating Agencies shall endeavor to provide sufficient telecommunications facilities to meet requirements of, and de-

mand for, international telecommunication services. For this purpose, and to ensure an adequate return on investment in high bandwidth infrastructures, operating agencies shall negotiate commercial agreements to achieve a sustainable system of fair compensation for telecommunications services and, where appropriate, respecting the principle of sending party network pays.

A non-voting member of the ITU, ETNO can, like any other entity, defend and push its ideas to all member states. The organization's argument appears reasonable in terms of principle, but is unacceptable to the US. A 'paying sender' principle would place the US in a premium position as a payer. The current situation is actually the opposite: in effect, a 'paying receiver' system. When, for example, a citizen of Botswana uses Google's search engine, the relevant operating agency of Botswana will ultimately have to pay the operator sending the data. Consequently, when a massive spam campaign is enacted, the consumption of bandwidth is assigned to the receivers. Few people realize that the largest share of spam is sent from servers based in the US. Naturally, these servers are paid for the service. Yet, this also creates a 'consumption of bandwidth' for the receivers, resulting in greater usage charges.

A New Payment Approach

Critically, the connections between more than 40,000 autonomous systems (nodes/servers) at a global level are ruled by contractual agreements between operating agencies. All are linked to a national territory and must deal with the regulations in their home jurisdiction. The commercial agreements between operating agencies are secret. It is very difficult—if not impossible—for a journalist, academic or public official to access such information. While video pricing is known, we still have no clear picture of the revenues flowing from the interconnections between bandwidth operators.

Switching to a model that combines both principles—that is, where sending and receiving parties each contribute to infrastructure costs—would modify the distribution of revenues between operating agencies. Most significantly, American actors would have to pay other national operators. Part of the redistribution could be used to assist emerging and developing countries develop broadband infrastructure, reducing the technological deficit and boosting economic growth. Google—amongst other big senders—would be unable to continue using freely 'collective global capital' (the worldwide infrastructure network) for which it did not spend a penny. The fact that Google is building its own CDN centers is not comparable, albeit the company's actions may indirectly help to resolve data 'traffic jams' by locating content closer to end users, and reducing the 'journey' of data packets. Amending the *ITR* to introduce a new payment approach would be revolutionary—a revolution not welcomed, however, by US interests.

The Fairy Tale of Internet Governance

Listening to the assembled US voices preaching against any changes at WCIT-12, a central argument is based around the notion of defending the Internet as a pure and perfect example of a democratic, decentralized system, allowing all users a controlling stake in some kind of balanced and participatory wonder. The old credo by David Clark in 1992—"we reject presidents, kings and voting; we believe in rough consensus and running code"—is part of the web wonderland hagiography, but not reflective of today's Internet reality. Even *The Economist* appears blind to the fairytale: "for something so central to the modern world, the Internet is shambolically governed. But sometimes chaos . . . is not disastrous: the Internet mostly works. And the shambles is a lot better than the alternative—which nearly always in this case means governments bringing the Internet under their control." The Internet works because it operates according to agreed principles, rules and centralized control—one must maintain a clear-eyed perspective.

Amongst the voices speaking in foreboding terms of potential WCIT-12 outcomes is Joe Waz, who co-wrote a blog in the *Huffington Post* with Phil Weiser, former Senior Advisor for Technology and Innovation to the National Economic Council's Director at the White House, and now Dean of Law at the University of Colorado. "The least understood or appreciated factor in the Internet's growth and success is its amazing capacity for self-governance, and its ability to resist the traditional tools of government regulation." This might be true when speaking about a web where users can create and participate in unlimited communities, websites or blogs, but this does not equate to control over the only critical command center of the Internet—its rooting system. Without the right IP, domain and link, the Internet goes nowhere.

The Power Fallacy

Despite the fact that the US government never really owned the Internet, it 'offered' control of its backbone and policy-generating function to a private Californian association—the Internet Corporation for Assigned Names and Numbers (ICANN)—that has engaged in activities representing "US governmental regulation in all but name" according to Michael Froomkin.

The first question one must ask is: how can you give something away that doesn't belong to you? The second: how do you maintain control once you've handed it over to friendly private entities? By controlling the private entities one would assume! Having done so, the cherry on the cake would be announcing to the public at large that the transfer of control from governmental to private hands should be viewed as a great success story. This is what happened in 1998, despite fierce resistance from Jon Postel. As one of the founding fathers of the Internet and 'ruler' of its early governance structure, Postel attempted to save the Internet from falling into the control of US government hands. Postel died, however, just weeks before the White House Special Advisor heading an ad hoc interagency task force on electronic commerce was able to claim full victory over the academics who were, until then, managing the central rooting system.

Postel entered the Internet Society's (ISOC) Hall of Fame in 2011, along with Vint Cerf, Google's 'Chief Internet Evangelist' and *cardinal des basses oeuvres* ["hatchet man"], now a key player in campaigning for the regulatory status quo. Ironically, Postel was nominated alongside Cerf. Similarly ironic—and tragic—was the fact that Ira Magaziner, the White House Special Advisor once depicted as Hillary Clinton's 'Rasputin', delivered a speech at Postel's memorial ceremony in Los Angeles in 1998, at the same time the US government officially transferred Internet governance powers to ICANN. Both Cerf and Magaziner were instrumental in the take-over. Foreseeing these developments, Postel himself had turned to the UN and ITU, but to no avail.

The Bad Guys

Constructing a fairytale usually requires a cast of 'bad guys.' Vladimir Putin declares that WCIT-12 should address Internet governance, and you get the plot line that Russia wants to control the Internet and its infrastructure networks. Ditto China. Finally, add the influence of Dr Hamadoun Touré, ITU's Malian Secretary-General who received his PhD in the former USSR, to the mix. Now we have all the necessary threads to point to a thinly-disguised attempt by the dark forces of totalitarianism to seize cyber control in the best Cold War style. What a nice (paranoid) story—supported by no substantive evidence.

Cyber Security

This brings us to the fourth issue identified at the outset— cyber security. Each of the US, Israel and Japan have developed official cyber military doctrines, though the US is by far the country with the largest budget devoted to digital or cyber war resources. Like air or naval power, the Pentagon has now added cyber power to its five major domains of military action. Eleanor Saitta, Technical Director of the International Modern Media Institute, has warned about the increasing militarization of the Internet. "Even as the 193 nations of the ITU meet in December, some will be silently unleashing state-sponsored cyber attacks upon each other, as well as mass surveillance and intervention targeting their own citizens".

Censorship

The fifth issue is censorship. As most are aware, any country today has the ability to control its own cyberspace, blocking or censoring any of its citizens. At the same time, censorship of Internet-based speech has proven difficult, as recent global tumult toppling repressive government regimes has shown. A Russian and Chinese proposal for a code of conduct serves to both challenge the US, as well as attempt to add legal weight to Moscow and Beijing's national censorship toolkits used to restrain citizen freedom. "It is obvious that this kind of proposal will have no support from the developed countries" acknowledges Alix Desforges, from the Institute Français de Géopolitique at Université Paris 8. "Today, countries prefer to sign bilateral agreements on security issues. We're miles away from international cooperation."

Touré himself emphasizes that according to the prevailing international regulatory framework, such national "restrictions are permitted by article 34 of the ITU's Constitution, which provides that the 193 member states reserve the right to cut off, in accordance with their national law, any private telecommunications which may appear dangerous to the security of the state, or contrary to its laws, to public order or to decency. And the *International Telecommunications Regulations* cannot contradict that provision, either."

A Global Campaign

With the clock ticking down to Dubai, Cerf is very busy coordinating a global campaign against any revision of the *ITR*. Only a few days ago he was video-linking with Sharan Burrow and Paul Twomey before an audience of international correspondents based in London. Twomey is a former ICANN CEO and President (2003-09). In 1997, as CEO of the National Office for the Information Economy, an Australian government unit developing Internet policy, he befriended Magaziner, leading to his initial involvement with the nascent ICANN. The two later partnered in a consultancy called Argo P@cificLondon. Burrow, also an Australian, is the Secretary General of the International Trade Union Confederation (ITUC)—strangely, a group now fighting against revision of the Melbourne treaty.

"An unfettered internet, free of political control and available to everyone could be relegated to cyber-history under a contentious proposal by a little known United Nations body" writes the *Equal Times*, an online publication of the ITUC. Burrow has launched a 'Stop the Net Grab' campaign, which has registered a little over 1,000 supporters (as of 18 November [2012]). She also convinced Kumi Naidoo, Executive Director of Greenpeace International, to co-sign a letter to the UN Secretary General, Ban Ki-moon, urging his intervention to maintain a "multi-stakeholder approach"—a view endorsed and supported by Cerf who has denied the legitimacy of governments in the context of Internet matters. According to Cerf, the Internet should be governed by rules set by "the Internet community," which rightly override national regulations. Such an approach would need much clarification. For instance, what would be the representative principles of such a community?

The Grey Zone

The grey zone where US officials and people like Cerf mingle is larger than meets the eye. There are many (disconcerting)

What Does ICANN Do?

To reach another person on the Internet you have to type an address into your computer—a name or a number. That address must be unique so computers know where to find each other. ICANN coordinates these unique identifiers across the world. Without that coordination, we wouldn't have one global Internet.

In more technical terms, the Internet Corporation for Assigned Names and Numbers (ICANN) coordinates the Domain Name System (DNS), Internet Protocol (IP) addresses, space allocation, protocol identifier assignment, generic (gTLD) and country code (ccTLD) Top-Level Domain name system management, and root server system management functions. These services were originally performed under U.S. Government contract by the Internet Assigned Numbers Authority (IANA) and other entities. ICANN now performs the IANA function.

ICANN, "About ICANN," 2013. www.icann.org.

examples. Take the Congressional hearing back in May [2012], which called upon the US to defend its position over the Internet and led to the approval of a bipartisan resolution opposing proposals in a "UN Forum." Before passing the resolution, three speakers participated in the hearing: Vint Cerf, Sally Shipman Wentworth, a senior manager at ISOC [Internet Society] and a former State Department official, and David A Gross, also a former State Department official turned lobbyist, representing all the major private sector players (including Google). Another example of Google's omnipotence is an article by a Google employee (Patrick S Ryan) published in the *Stanford Technology Law Review*, which strongly attacks the WCIT-12 process, the ITU and any envisaged reform of the ITR.

Ultimately, all Cerf's efforts may only end up focusing more attention on the current 'non-democratic' nature of Internet governance, as well as the associated inequalities of the business side of the web. They may also raise legitimate concerns over Google's power to finance behind-the-scenes maneuvering to preserve a favorable regulatory environment. Google is a giant of email, personal data, mobile telephony, content diffusion, cloud computing, the digitalization of books, intellectual property rights, search engines and advertising revenues, aggressively aggregates media content, and exploits global telecommunications network infrastructure without contributing to costs. A handful of countries like Germany and France are now launching legal action on behalf of their content producers and Internet users to stop these strong-arm tactics.

As WCIT-12 approaches, it is clear that telecommunications networks are entering the fray, ready to fight for their own future. On the media front, the issue goes far beyond the fact that over 80 percent of global digital revenues flow to Google and Facebook. Democracy requires independent media. Almost all are now lost to the law of the click for the sake of being seen by Google News, while dreaming of catching a scrap of Google's leftover advertising revenues. We all know about these developments, but feign to ignore them. Even amongst the most prominent human rights defenders one can observe a surprising attitude: every month Amnesty International UK's Head of Marketing spends approximately US $10,000 to secure key words to link to the NGO's website. One can only wonder how much money Amnesty International contributes on a global level to Google's deep pockets, which bulged to the tune of nearly US $38 billion in revenue in 2011 alone.

Democracy is at stake, when many of us are asleep or comforting ourselves with benign fairytales.

> *"The real issue [is] whether member governments can use the UN to hijack the Internet agenda."*

The United Nations Should Not Govern the Internet

Arthur Herman

Arthur Herman is an author and journalist. In the following viewpoint, he maintains that Internet governance proposals discussed at the 2012 World Conference on Internet Telecommunications (WCIT-12) in Dubai, United Emirates, are tantamount to a power grab. Herman argues that authoritarian countries are attempting to transfer Internet governance from the United States and private independent companies to the United Nations, an international body he characterizes as besieged by financial and political scandal. Herman warns that the Internet is at a crossroads, and if the attempt succeeds, access to the Internet will be significantly damaged: authoritarian countries will be able to limit access and practice Internet censorship unchallenged. Western countries, Herman insists, must not be intimidated by charges of cultural bias and stand steadfast in their commitment to a free and democratic Internet—and that means resisting any efforts to allow the United Nations to play a greater role its in governance.

As you read, consider the following questions:

1. When does Herman say that the conflict over Internet governance began?

2. As reported by the author, who invented the hyperlink system known as the World Wide Web?

3. What year was the Internet Corporation for Assigned Names and Numbers (ICANN) created, according to Herman?

Leo Tolstoy once said, "Imagine Genghis Khan with a telephone." Imagine Genghis Khan, or a gaggle of Genghis Khans, running the Internet, and you have a sense of the ideas that will be percolating in Dubai at the World Conference on International Telecommunications in December [2012].

Delegates from 120 countries will gather under the auspices of the United Nations to consider a plan to take administrative control of the Internet away from the United States and hand it over to an international body run by the UN.

In short, governance of cyberspace will pass from the country that has kept it free and accessible since its creation—the United States—to the same organization that gave us the financial scandals at UNESCO [United Nations Educational, Scientific, and Cultural Organization], voted to designate Zionism as racism, and seated China, Syria, and Muammur Qaddafi's Libya on its Commission on Human Rights.

A Defining Moment

"The Internet stands at a crossroads," is how Vint Cerf, one of the Web's founders, put it in a May [2012] *New York Times* opinion piece. What happens in Dubai, he wrote, could "take away the Internet as you and I have known it." Those who share his concern cross the ideological divide. Rebecca MacKinnon, of the liberal New America Foundation, and former [George W.] Bush administration officials, such as

Ambassador David Gross, similarly see Dubai as a defining moment, especially because the driving forces behind the meeting's agenda are Russia and China. Those two nations have established themselves as the world's worst cybercrime offenders and most systematic suppressers of political dissent on the Internet.

Whoever controls the Internet controls the destiny of nations. Ultimately, how Internet governance gets settled in Dubai and afterward could well determine whether freedom or totalitarianism gains the upper hand in the 21st century.

The Origins of the Conflict

This all began in 2005, when the United Nations sponsored a World Summit on the Information Society (WSIS) in Tunis. That choice of venue was itself rich with irony, since Tunisia's then dictator, Zine El Abidine Ben Ali, was the Arab world's leading censor of the Internet, and the two sponsors of the summit's trade fair were China's biggest network companies, Huawei and ZTE. They are the anchors of China's Great Firewall that keeps out Western ideas and suppresses dissent—and also leaves it free to hack into the secrets of Western governments and corporations more or less at will.

That is precisely the kind of Internet many other countries would like to have, and China emerged from the Tunis meeting as their chief spokesman. Several belong to the so-called G-77 of developing countries, which includes Pakistan, the Philippines, Brazil, and Argentina, as well as Iran, Syria, and Venezuela. They believe that the administration of the World Wide Web by the Internet Corporation for Assigned Names and Numbers (ICANN), headquartered in Los Angeles, isn't responsive enough to the needs of developing countries, and so they pushed through a paragraph in the Tunis final report that "underlines the need to maximize the participation of developing countries in decisions regarding Internet governance, which *should* reflect their interests, as well as in development and capacity building"—in other words, in helping governments control what their citizens can see, and can't see, on the Internet.

The best way to do that, China proposed in the run-up to the Tunis meeting, was to take administrative control of the Internet away from ICANN and hand it over to the International Telecommunication Union (ITU). The Union is a branch of the United Nations in which all countries have an equal vote, whether their delegates know anything about the Internet or not. (Most of the calls made by ICANN are done by engineers who have a background in cyber issues, and who are also—inevitably—trained and educated in the West).

A Gathering Storm

A clear agenda was taking shape, with Chinese help. Free and open access to the Internet was being defined as a "Western" or "Eurocentric" priority that should not be imposed on "developing countries" by a Western institution such as ICANN. Accepting censorship as a governing principle was being defined as showing sensitivity to the needs of the developing world—with a UN-based body as the perfect vehicle for doing it.

Some human-rights groups disagreed. "If we have no freedom of speech," said one WSIS delegate, a dissident from Zimbabwe, "we can't talk about who is stealing our food." But what began in Tunis reached a crescendo in September 2011 in Nairobi, [Kenya,] where 2,000 delegates from 100 countries met for an Internet Governance Forum (IGF) under UN auspices. There, Russia rallied around the idea of passing control over to the ITU as well. According to President Vladimir Putin, the goal of the IGF should be "establishing international control over the Internet," meaning that national governments, not users, would have the final say in the "norms and rules ... concerning information and cyberspace." Not only

China, but also Iran, India, Brazil, and South Africa have signed on to the International Telecommunication Union plan.

Nor is the ITU's current secretary general, Hamadoun Touré, opposed. He graduated from the Technical Institute of Leningrad and Moscow Tech in the Soviet era, and he knows the case against free speech only too well. But he also knows how to couch the case for Internet takeover in terms acceptable to Western liberals.

Buzzwords

One term is *democracy*. As Touré told *Vanity Fair*, "When an invention becomes used by billions across the world, it no longer remains the sole property of one nation"—meaning the United States. "There should be a mechanism where many countries have an opportunity to have a say. I think that's democratic. Do you think that's democratic?"

Another buzzword is *security*. Everyone worries about proliferation of cybercrime and unauthorized hacking. Just before the Nairobi meeting commenced, Russia and China, backed by Tajikistan and Uzbekistan, called for creating an International Code of Conduct for Information Security, ostensibly aimed at curtailing cybercrimes such as hacking and terrorism. One of the code's provisions would be committing signatories to "curbing the dissemination of information which incites terrorism, secessionism, extremism or undermines other countries' political, economic, and social stability."

The goal, in short, will be to force the United States, Canada, and Europe to shut down dissident websites or sites that provide any information another government deems extreme or antisocial. Most Arab countries at the Dubai meeting will go along with this goal, especially in the wake of the Arab Spring, when they learned what can happen if citizens have even limited access to the Web and social-networking sites such as Facebook and Twitter.

The Cultural-Bias Argument

Another key appeal is on multiculturalist grounds. ICANN's business is largely conducted in English, and until recently the domain names it generated used the Latin alphabet (now they're available in Arabic, Chinese, and a host of other languages and characters). Critics such as the Internet Governance Project [IGP] have long argued that the organization has a pro-Western, even pro-American bias. The group even states on its website that "the United States government holds unilateral control of critical Internet resources," meaning ICANN, "against the will of users and governments in Europe, Asia, Latin America, and Africa."

One could argue, on the other hand, that this alleged tilt toward Western values is something many dissidents in China and Iran might desperately want to increase—just as they probably have a clearer notion of who's being held against his will, or who's not, than the IGP does. Still, the diversity argument has many sincere proponents, and the fact is, the United States and Western countries are a major source of the information that authoritarian regimes and others in the developing world find objectionable (as witness the tremendous furor recently over the *Innocence of Muslims* video).

Concerns About the UN

But handing control over such content to the UN is where even a liberal critic like Rebecca MacKinnon has to draw the line. Former CNN correspondent, author of *Consent of the Networked*, and an enthusiast for "democratizing" the Internet, MacKinnon is no fan of ICANN or what she sees as the preponderant role corporate sponsors play in its decisions. Still, she recognizes how China has cleverly used the cultural-bias argument to push for replacing the current "multi-stake holder" model of cyberspace—in which governments have no more say than do engineers, activist groups, and the technology companies who own its biggest servers—with one in which governments will dominate. And many of those governments, she notes, don't have the consent of their own citizens.

"The UN system's chronic inability to protect and uphold human rights around the world," she writes, "and its propensity to empower and legitimize dictators within the global governance system—as well as the lack of technical understanding of how the Internet really works among many countries' ministers of communications—are good reasons that power over the Internet's critical resources should be kept out of intergovernmental hands," and in the hands of ICANN.

In fact, contrary to the multicultural critics, one could argue the key to the success of the Internet lies precisely in its original, American, even capitalist, bias.

History of the Internet

The widely circulated story that the Pentagon created the Internet to keep vital computer communications open in the event of a nuclear strike is a myth. The original network built by the Defense Department's Advanced Research Projects Agency (DARPA) in the late 1960s had nothing to do with nukes—it was to ease communication among universities doing defense-related research—and was funded, not built, by the government. Nearly all the technology involved, including the first computer hardware and phone lines, was installed by private companies such as Honeywell and AT&T—and when ARPA's director, Robert Taylor, moved to Xerox, that company developed the first Ethernet to connect different private computer networks.

Indeed, the explosive growth of what had been a government research project has been steadily fueled by U.S. corporations such as CompuServe, universities, and individual engineers such as Stanford's Vint Cerf, the inventor of the TCP/IP address system, as well as Britain's Tim Berners-Lee, who in 1990 developed the hyperlink system he dubbed the World Wide Web. The Internet is the one clear, simple, and efficient

---

Countries That Practice Internet Censorship

Countries Classified as "Enemies of the Internet"

Bahrain	North Korea
Belarus	Saudi Arabia
Burma	Syria
China	Turkmenistan
Cuba	Uzbekistan
Iran	Vietnam

Countries "Under Surveillance" for Troubling Internet Censorship Practices

Australia	Russia
Egypt	South Korea
Eritrea	Sri Lanka
France	Thailand
India	Tunisia
Kazakhstan	Turkey
Malaysia	United Arab Emirates

TAKEN FROM: Reporters Without Borders, "Internet Enemies Report 2012," en.rsf.org.

---

communications network that everyone depends on, regardless of national origin or ideological orientation. That's why most American companies who do business on the Internet support the work of open-standards organizations such as the Internet Engineering Task Force and World Wide Web Consortium, as well as ICANN. All three are nonprofit voluntary organizations that answer to no government and state in their charters that they serve the interests of Web users.

The Triumph of the Internet

By the time ICANN was created in 1998, the Internet had spread from the United States to more than 100 countries. Today it includes some 2 billion users, sharing millions of bytes of data and information every second. Everyone recognizes that it is a truly global institution with no government master. But it also retains its fundamental American character, as a never-ending cascade of what Cerf calls "permissionless innovation." Users from all over the world are constantly adding to and extending its performance, not to mention its range of services and commodities and new ideas. It is "not merely a radiance of connections; it is a mesh of constant invention," writes George Gilder in his book *Telecosm*. "The Internet is yet another demonstration of the triumph of intelligence over time and chaos"—and of the profoundly American principle that freedom is superior to constraint and control.

The Role of ICANN

International bodies such as the Internet Engineering Task Force are important to keeping the Web strong, efficient, and open, but ICANN is crucial. Its job is to oversee the assignment of the unique identifiers essential for the TCP/IP address system. By making sure every computer server or network has a unique Information Protocol address, ICANN is able to ensure that any user gets access to data emanating from that specific address and no other—and can do so from anywhere he or she enters that address on a Web browser, whether it's to look at a website, download data, send an email, or buy something.

It also makes sure that the number of available domain names and addresses keeps up with the expansion of the Internet—which is one of the issues that has already led to some friction with governments, including that of the United States. Indeed, if ICANN has any "bias" at all, it is in expanding the Internet and making it more available to users, no matter who or where they are, according to certain rules of the road called the Internet Technical Regulations, set down in an international conference in Melbourne back in 1988.

With ICANN as umpire, the Internet has become the closest thing to a globalized free market the world has ever seen, where individuals anywhere are able to use a basic and neutral set of rules to match their preferences—including buying and selling goods and services. Like any free market, the Internet is subject to abuse and prey to predators, both governmental and nongovernmental. But as the commissioner of the Federal Communications Commission, Robert McDowell, notes, thanks to ICANN, the Internet has become "the greatest deregulatory success story of all time."

Changing the Rules

Others, of course, view that deregulatory narrative not as a success story but as a threat—especially the authoritarian governments who would much prefer having an Internet they can directly police. (Iran, for example, has announced plans to create its own "clean" or halal Internet, which will serve individuals and institutions inside Iran in accordance with Sharia law and remain entirely cut off from the World Wide Web.) But they see replacing ICANN outright with a UN agency subject to their control as politically unfeasible—and also too much work. So they're looking at a different route. Instead of firing the umpire, they want to seize the rulebook by which he operates. And the place they intend to do that is Dubai.

After the December conference, "the governments of the world will have more power over the Internet than ever before," warns David Gross, who coordinated the State Department's communications policy under George W. Bush. What Gross expects is the creation of a new framework under the auspices of the International Telecommunication Union—in which nation-states will make the important calls on changing the rules of the road, the International Telecommunication Regulations. These are "the most important and sensitive aspects" of how the Internet is organized, or rather, how it runs itself.

One of those changes would be taking dominion over ICANN's assignment of identities for the origin and destination of Internet traffic. This could allow governments to force ICANN to erase domains or IP addresses they don't like, thereby cutting them permanently from the Internet and dumping them down the cybersphere's memory hole.

Another would be inserting the Chinese- and Russian-sponsored International Code of Conduct for Information Security into the Internet's rules, which would force its international custodians, including ICANN, to cooperate with governments that want to censor what flows into their country.

Payment Schemes Threaten Access

The third would radically alter who pays for using the Internet. The Dubai conference will weigh proposals that invoke the principle of "sender party pays," making content providers such as Google and Yahoo! purchase the right to transmit content to users. "It's a completely new economic concept to the Internet," says Gross, "and it could have a radical and profound impact on the economics of the Internet, especially in the developing world."

The example he likes to use is a poor student in a village in Thailand or Nigeria who wants to download a page from a website he found on Google. As the Internet currently works, he gets the information for free: The only cost is paying for the Internet connection in the host country. "But if Google had to pay someone for the right to send that information," Gross says, that person might decide not to send it at all. "The eyeballs of a rural person in Thailand to an advertiser aren't probably worth the trouble." The result would be to shut down or severely limit access to the Internet in the world's poorest places—something that several governments might not find so objectionable.

Nor would its effects be limited to places like Thailand and Nigeria. Gross anticipates that "sender party pays" would lead to a multitiered World Wide Web, with different data provided to different users based on their levels of income and on advertising rates. That's not just a crimp to commerce; it spells an end of Internet democracy.

Old Tensions Resurface

Gross's fears, like Rebecca MacKinnon's, are rooted in the Internet's possible future. But there's another older story being played out in Dubai, one familiar even to people who still haven't decided whether the Internet is a good thing for the culture or not.

Given that Russia and China are prime movers in the bid to wrest Internet oversight from the United States; that their allies include Iran, Syria, and Venezuela; and that ITU's Touré was trained and taught by Soviet apparatchiks [government bureaucrats], it's hard to resist the feeling we're watching a replay of the North–South debates of the 1970s, when totalitarians used the issue of the inequality of nations to push their real agenda of undermining the power of the United States and the West—not because they were barriers to prosperity, democracy, and free expression, but because they were their chief exponents.

As [the late senator from New York] Daniel Patrick Moynihan wrote then: "Our policymakers have yet to learn just how dangerous the world [has] become for a nation like ours, or to see that guarding the language of human rights would play no small part in our defense." Substitute "Internet" for "language of human rights," and one has a very clear statement of what's at stake in the Internet-governance debate.

Assessing the Threat

It's not at all clear that the officials who will handle the Dubai issue for the [Barack] Obama administration understand this. A memo issued by the State Department on January 23, 2012, after the Nairobi meeting dismissed the idea that a takeover of the Internet was in the offing. "There are no pending proposals to invest the ITU with ICANN-like government authority," it states—ignoring the fact that the real issue in Dubai will not be whether the UN agency replaces ICANN but whether member governments can use the UN to hijack the Internet agenda and reduce ICANN to a mere administrator of their collective will.

The same memo insists that the Obama administration must continue to support open access to the Internet and stresses that its efforts to push further "liberalization of international telecommunications networks" would be completely successful at Dubai. But it's not likely that an administration whose response to Muslim outrage over an allegedly derogatory video on YouTube was to seize and detain its producer is going to be a strong advocate for free speech—or for keeping the Internet free from nation-state control.

The Internet has proven that creativity and innovation flourish best when governments govern least. The United States has a solemn duty to protect the legacy it founded. In that sense, he who controls the Internet does control the destiny of nations—and ultimately the destiny of freedom.

> *"The biggest threats to Internet freedom today . . . come from national governments."*

US Government Control of the Internet Threatens Freedom

Milton L. Mueller

Milton L. Mueller is a professor at Syracuse University School of Information Studies. In the following viewpoint, he argues that the greatest threat to the Internet is national governments seeking Internet sovereignty for the purposes of limiting access and imposing Internet censorship. Mueller contends that the fears of a United Nations takeover of the Internet are foolish and trumped up by the United States in order to keep and expand its global reach. He points out that such concerns are a deflection from more significant issues, including Internet security, widespread surveillance, and stifling regulations.

As you read, consider the following questions:

1. What does Mueller compare to the hype surrounding the WCIT-12 in Dubai?

Milton L. Mueller, "Greatest Threat to the Internet: Governments," *San Francisco Chronicle*, July 20, 2012. Copyright © 2012 by Milton L. Mueller. All rights reserved. Reproduced by permission.

2. As described by the author, what is Stuxnet?

3. According to a report by the *New York Times*, as cited by Mueller, how many government demands for subscriber information did cell phone carriers respond to in 2011?

When U.S. politicians and businesses tell us that the revision of the International Telecommunication Regulations could lead to a takeover of the Internet or global censorship, I think of [Iraqi dictator] Saddam Hussein.

Why Hussein? The invasion of Iraq was based on the claim that the Iraqi dictator held weapons of mass destruction [WMD], and thus posed a clear and present danger to this country and the world. Those who wanted a war played up the threats to manufacture political support. We now know that there were no WMD; we were rushed into war under false pretenses. The result, most agree, was disastrous. Here's the lesson I hope we all learned: a false diagnosis, inflated to provoke extreme, hasty action, leads to bad outcomes. Something very similar to the WMD claims seems to characterize our approach to the World Conference of International Telecommunications (or WCIT, pronounced "wicket").

Maybe the stakes seem lower. No one thinks millions of people are going to die because of an International Telecommunication Union meeting in Dubai.

But from another perspective the stakes are much higher.

An Implausible Scenario

The linkage of powerful information technology to free, open, global communications makes gigantic contributions to civilization and commerce. And it was the Internet—the ability to network computers across borders, free from nation-state controls and permissions—that opened up this new world for us. If that is truly threatened by WCIT, it is indeed something to rise up about.

But the claim that the revision of the International Tele-communication Regulations constitutes a mortal threat to the future of the Internet is absurd. It is even less plausible than the claim that Hussein was harboring WMD.

The simple fact is that the WCIT cannot possibly undo the Internet revolution unless all the governments involved, including the United States, agree to do so. The International Telecommunication Union has no police force, no army. It cannot make any state do something it doesn't want to do. It cannot even fine or tax corporations. There is no Internet-WMD hidden in its stately offices in Geneva [Switzerland]. Internet governance is not even the main target of the current WCIT negotiations.

The Biggest Threats to the Internet

The biggest threats to Internet freedom today do not come from intergovernmental organizations. They come from national governments with the institutional mechanisms to regulate, restrict, surveil, censor and license Internet suppliers and users. National governments have police forces, armies—and armies of regulators. This includes, especially, our own government, which has greater global reach than any other state.

As for China and Russia, they do not need the International Telecommunication Union or the union's WCIT to restrict their citizens' communications and use of the Internet. They are already doing it.

Key Questions

So why is so much attention being focused on a relatively obscure Internet governance process? Aren't there other, more important, things to worry about? Before getting exercised about WCIT, here are some things we need to ask our own government:

- What are the long-term implications of our development and release of dangerous cyber weapons such as Stuxnet? Could U.S. initiatives lead to militarization or national partition of the Internet?

- If we want to keep governments' hands off the Internet, why has the U.S. Commerce Department insisted on giving the Internet Corporation for Assigned Names and Numbers' (ICANN) Governmental Advisory Committee—whose members are exactly the same as the International Telecommunication Union's—more authority over domain-name policy, including the power to object to any new top-level domain names it doesn't like?

- If we want to keep governments' hands off the Internet, why is our Federal Communications Commission proposing to tax foreign telecom carriers to subsidize universal service in this country?

- Will there be any limits to the orgy of surveillance that domestic law enforcement agencies are conducting through the mobile-phone system? (*The New York Times* has reported that cell phone carriers responded to 1.3 million government demands for subscriber information last year [2011].) Will this surveillance be extended to the global domain name system via ICANN, which collects contact information when a domain name is registered, as U.S. law enforcement agencies are currently demanding?

- Will the defeated Stop Online Piracy Act legislation return, or will there be any similar attempts to flex regulatory muscles internationally on behalf of big copyright owners? Should we be as worried about the World Intellectual Property Organization and the Motion Picture Association of America as we are about the International Telecommunication Union?

- Will the United States continue to intensify its leverage over financial choke points as an instrument of Internet policy, as exhibited in the cases of online gambling and WikiLeaks? Are these centralized regulatory tools consistent with the Internet model of decentralized control?

Sure, the International Telecommunication Union is a pre-Internet bureaucracy and some of its member-states would love to restrict communications or protect their local monopolies from Internet-based competition. But those kinds of threats existed before the WCIT and will continue after it.

I am less worried about what will happen in Dubai than I am about what is happening in Washington.

> *"I believe that the multi-stakeholder approach to Internet governance and technical management has been, and will continue to be, the best way to address the technical and policy issues facing the Internet globally."*

A Multistakeholder Global Coalition Should Govern the Internet

Vinton Cerf

Vinton Cerf is a computer scientist, the founding president of the Internet Society, a former chairman of the Internet Corporation for Assigned Names and Numbers (ICANN), and a vice president and "chief Internet evangelist" at Google. He is well known as an Internet pioneer. In the following viewpoint, taken from congressional testimony, he asserts that the multistakeholder approach to Internet governance is the most effective way to keep the Internet functioning and to guarantee access to more people worldwide. It is crucial for the US government to engage like-minded countries at the 2012 World Conference on International Telecommunications (WCIT-12) in Dubai in order to organize a global coalition to protect this approach to Internet governance,

Vinton Cerf, "International Proposals to Regulate the Internet," US House of Representatives Energy and Commerce Committee, May 31 2012.

Cerf contends. In this effort, he explains, transparency and accountability are key. The UN's International Telecommunication Union (ITU) is quite capable of suggesting policy principles and assisting in capacity building, Cerf concludes, but it should not adopt nor impose Internet regulations.

As you read, consider the following questions:

1. According to a May 2011 study by the McKinsey Global Institute, cited by Cerf, how much money exchanges hands each year through e-commerce?

2. What does the author describe as the function of the Internet Governance Forum (IGF)?

3. Why did the United Nations list Internet penetration in its Millennium Development Goals, according to Cerf?

As one of the "fathers of the Internet" and as a computer scientist, I care deeply about issues relating to the Internet's infrastructure. This is why I am grateful for the opportunity to testify before your Subcommittee on the critically important issue of international Internet governance and regulation.

The Internet and the World Wide Web have generated an unprecedented explosion in commerce and creativity. According to a May 2011 study by the McKinsey Global Institute ("Internet Matters: The net's sweeping impact on growth, jobs, and prosperity"), nearly $8 trillion exchange hands each year through e-commerce. The same report states that the Internet accounts for 21 percent of gross domestic product growth in the last five years in mature countries, and that the benefits are not reserved for Internet companies—in fact, 75 percent of Internet economic impact benefits companies that are not pure Internet players.

And a March 2012 report by the Boston Consulting Group—entitled "The Internet Economy in the G-20: The

$4.2 Trillion Growth Opportunity"—provides policy makers more data about the impact of the Internet on economic growth and job creation. According to the report, Internet-savvy small- and medium-sized enterprises (SME) across eleven of the G-20 countries [i.e., those twenty countries with the largest economies] have experienced 22 percent higher revenue growth over the last three years than comparable businesses with no Internet usage. The report also found that SMEs that have an Internet presence generate more jobs. In Germany, for example, 93 percent of companies that were heavy users of the Internet and web services increased employment over the past three years, compared with only 50 percent of their offline competitors.

A Threat to the Internet

But today, despite the significant positive impact of the Internet on the world's economy, this amazing technology stands at a crossroads. The Internet's success has generated a worrying desire by some countries' governments to create new international rules that would jeopardize the network's innovative evolution and its multi-faceted success.

This effort is manifesting itself in the UN General Assembly and at the International Telecommunication Union—the ITU—a United Nations organization that counts 193 countries as its members, each holding one vote. The ITU currently is conducting a review of the international agreements governing telecommunications and it aims to expand its regulatory authority to include the Internet at a treaty summit scheduled for December of this year [2012] in Dubai.

Such a move holds profound—and I believe potentially hazardous—implications for the future of the Internet and all of its users. If all of us do not pay attention to what is going on, users worldwide will be at risk of losing the open and free Internet that has brought so much to so many.

In my testimony this morning I will address this effort at the ITU and make three broad observations and recommendations:

- First, I believe that the multi-stakeholder approach to Internet governance and technical management has been, and will continue to be, the best way to address the technical and policy issues facing the Internet globally.

- Second, it is critically important for the United States Government to engage in the ITU process and encourage like-minded countries—those that believe in the social and economic benefits of a free and open Internet—to do so as well. We need a global coalition to ensure transparency, openness, and an outcome that preserves the features of the Internet and its operation that have been so productive over the past 30 years.

- Finally, the very real concerns about the damage that ITU regulation could do to the Internet should not minimize the existing concerns that developing nations have as they try to keep up with the 21st century economy. We can and should solve problems of access and education without compromising the Internet's essential open and decentralized character.

The Internet and the ITU

After its inception as a U.S. Government project, the Internet has been decentralized to maximize the effectiveness of the open, bottom-up, multi-stakeholder approach that has enabled unprecedented growth and innovation. This system was formally recognized in 2005 at the UN World Summit on the Information Society, and I believe it remains the right approach.

Many others agree. As the Organization for Economic Cooperation and Development noted in its December 2011 Rec-

Regulating Global Internet

ommendation on Principles for Internet Policy Making, the multi-stakeholder model provides "the flexibility and global scalability needed to address Internet policy challenges."

Many multi-stakeholder organizations have played a fundamental role in Internet governance and evolution. These include the non-profit ICANN [Internet Corporation for Assigned Names and Numbers], that oversees the handling of domain names, the Internet numeric address space, and the unique parameters needed for Internet standards; the Internet Architecture Board; and the Internet Engineering Task Force under the auspices of the Internet Society (ISOC), that develops and promotes technical standards via a series of volunteer-led working groups.

A recent and important adjunct to the multi-stakeholder institutions already associated with the Internet's governance is the UN's Internet Governance Forum (IGF). Created in Tunis in 2005, the IGF includes representatives from academia, civil society, governments, and the private sector. It is a highly democratic forum that enables the open expression of interests and discussion of concerns regarding the Internet, which can then be addressed by the appropriate expert body.

Of course, there is still room for improvement. For example, although ICANN has representatives from all world regions on its board, more international voices could be added. Similarly, although the IGF is already an open forum, it could do more to encourage and facilitate diverse groups, especially in the developing world, to participate in debate.

But if there's one thing that we should not do, it is to centralize decision-making power. The greatest strength of the current system of Internet governance is its meritocratic democracy. Anyone who cares can voice ideas and opinions, but the ultimate decisions are governed by broad consensus. It might not always be the most convenient of systems, but it's the fairest, safest, and historically most effective way to ensure that good ideas win out and bad ideas die.

Despite the benefits, there is a strong effort to put in place a system that stands in sharp contrast to the multi-stakeholder process.

Dangerous Proposals

Today, the ITU focuses on telecommunication networks, radio frequency allocation, and infrastructure development. But some powerful member countries see an opportunity to create regulatory authority over the Internet. Last June [2011], the Russian government stated its goal of establishing international control over the Internet through the ITU. Then, last September, the Shanghai Cooperation Organization—which counts China, Russia, Tajikistan, and Uzbekistan among its members—submitted a proposal to the UN General Assembly for an "International Code of Conduct for Information Security." The organization's stated goal was to establish government-led "international norms and rules standardizing the behavior of countries concerning information and cyberspace." Other proposals of a similar character have emerged from India and Brazil. And in an October 2010 meeting in Guadalajara, Mexico, the ITU itself adopted a specific proposal to "increase the role of ITU in Internet governance."

Several other proposals from member states would dramatically limit free expression on the web. Others would subject cyber security and data privacy to international control, and allow foreign phone companies to charge fees for international Internet traffic—perhaps on a "per-click" basis.

As a result of these efforts, there is a strong possibility that this December the ITU will significantly amend the International Telecommunication Regulations—a multilateral treaty last revised in 1988—in a way that authorizes increased ITU and member state control over the Internet. These proposals, if implemented, would change the foundational structure of the Internet that has historically led to unprecedented worldwide innovation and economic growth.

Because the ITU answers only to its member states—rather than to citizens, civil society, academia, the tech industry, and the broader private sector—there's a great need to insert transparency and accountability into this process and to prevent expansion of ITU or UN authority over the operation of the Internet.

A U.S. Partnership with Other Nations

It is critically important that the United States Government engage in the ITU process and encourage like-minded countries, NGOs [nongovernmental organizations], private-sector actors, and technical and civil society organizations that believe in the social and economic benefits of a free and open Internet to do so as well. We need a global and united coalition to ensure openness and an outcome that preserves the features of Internet development, governance, and operation that have produced economic, scientific, educational, and societal benefits for three decades.

To be clear, I do not believe that this is a challenge that the U.S. can meet on its own, but it is one that cannot be overcome without the leadership and engagement of the U.S. Government on three specific fronts: (1) promoting existing multi-stakeholder structures as much preferable alternatives to the centralization proposal of the ITU, (2) demonstrating for participating countries the tremendous benefits of the Internet as we know it today without the restrictions of an ITU or UN sanctioned global Internet treaty, and (3) ensuring an open and accountable process at the ITU so that the world understands the motivations and consequences of the ITU process.

Fostering Strong Alternatives

As part of its engagement with the ITU and other international organizations, the U.S. Government should emphasize that best way to address concerns from countries is to work through the system of transparent, democratic oversight organizations that is already in place for discussing and helping to resolve issues relating to the Internet.

As I've noted above, there are great benefits stemming from and tremendous support for multi-stakeholder structures like the Internet Governance Forum (IGF). Like the ITU, it is part of the UN structure. It is highly democratic and requires participation from academia, civil society, governments, and the private sector.

We also need to work together to create and refine voluntarily developed codes of conduct. A U.S.-based non-profit called the Global Network Initiative (GNI) is a great example. Google, along with a handful of other companies, human rights organizations, investors, and academics spent two years negotiating and creating a collaborative approach to protect freedom of expression and privacy in the ICT [information and communications technology] sector. The principles were published, and the GNI reports annually regarding how well its members uphold its standards.

There are few losers for these types of agreements. Companies and governments build public trust and gain insights from other stakeholders. Users get valuable information from the reports, and added protection from potential threats.

This is not to say that the current multi-stakeholder system is perfect or that it doesn't need reform. As I note above, there will always be room for improvement and it is up to everyone within the Internet community to participate in this process to continue to make the process better. For example, although ICANN has representatives from all world regions on its board, more international voices could be added and they can continue to improve on their processes to make them more transparent, accountable, and open. Similarly, although the IGF is already an open forum, it could do more to encourage and facilitate diverse groups, especially in the developing world, to participate in the debate.

The Tremendous Benefits of the Internet

I've referenced data indicating the significant economic benefits generated by the Internet. It's critical for the U.S. and other countries that have seen the positive impact of the Internet on their economies to highlight to ITU participants and other stakeholders the potential negative consequences of ITU regulation of the Internet on the world's economy.

Adding regulatory authority to the ITU—for example the ability to levy charges for international Internet traffic—could significantly hurt commerce. Small and medium U.S. businesses—indeed, small and medium businesses everywhere—are also important job creators, and we do not want to stifle their ability to grow by limiting the markets that they can reach.

Openness and Accountability

One of the key concerns I have with the ITU's process is that it is neither transparent nor sufficiently open to non-governmental stakeholders—conditions that result in insufficient accountability.

Today, a number of civil society organizations from around the world are joining to ask the ITU for more transparency as it considers various proposals that would result in its power to regulate the Internet on a global basis.

Concerns about transparency stem not from theoretical concerns but from actual experience. The preparatory process for the ITU's meeting in Dubai has been opaque, with significant restrictions on access to documents and high barriers to ITU membership. In fact, most member states of the ITU have not even opened public dialogues with Internet stakeholders to guide the development of their national positions or to seek input on their proposals. Many proposals go beyond merely technical interoperability of telecommunications infrastructure and would impact free expression, security, and other important issues.

As a result, a number of leaders in the human rights and free expression communities from around the world have signed a letter to call into question the ITU's barriers to participation: "The continued success of the information society depends on the full, equal, and meaningful participation of civil society stakeholders (alongside the private sector, the academic and technical community, and governments) in . . . both technical and public policy issues."

Transparency and openness are critical issues and we raise them here because it is important for parties to fully understand a process that affects all Internet users. Nevertheless, transparency alone is not enough to transform the ITU into a true multi-stakeholder organization.

The Concerns of Developing Nations

Only two billion of the world's seven billion people currently have access to the Internet. The UN in its Millennium Development Goals lists Internet penetration as a key metric in efforts to reduce poverty and encourage rational development, and expanding access need to be a priority. The data I outlined earlier regarding GDP [gross domestic product] growth and overall economic impact only highlight the importance of bringing access to those who do not yet have it.

Many countries believe that the ITU will help put policies in place that will promote development of broadband in developing countries. The ITU's Development program has done great work in developing countries to help promote broadband deployment, such as the Connect the World regional summits. Nevertheless, it is one thing for the ITU to suggest policy principles and assist in capacity building; it is quite another to adopt detailed regulations in this space. And the former can continue without the latter.

Rather, the ITU's development efforts ought to proceed in tandem with a vast number of national policies, public-private partnerships, and technical/non-profit community efforts to improve access and education in developing countries.

For example, ISOC has demonstrated the benefits of building Internet Exchange Points in Kenya and Nigeria. Google was involved in the Nigeria project, and it has supported the establishment and growth of Internet exchanges in the eastern Caribbean and the Middle East. We have also engaged in a number of other initiatives to increase access to the Internet in the developing world including building a proof-of-concept open access Wi-Fi network in Nairobi, Kenya. Google has been an active supporter of the Network Startup Resources Center at the University of Oregon, providing equipment, funding and volunteer staff to assist in its capacity building efforts that span over two decades.

We believe that education is also an important component of the effort to get more of the developing world online. Over the past two years Google has worked with the market research firm Basis Research Ltd in six key African countries (Ghana, Kenya, Nigeria, Senegal, South Africa, and Uganda) to understand how and why consumers in those countries use the Internet, or conversely why they are not online. The most prevalent reason for not going online was lack of knowledge—everything from not knowing what the Internet has to offer to not knowing how or where to get online. Lack of access was a close second. The survey results are available for free to the public at www.insightsafrica.com.

There clearly is a significant need to educate consumers in regions like Sub-Saharan Africa about how to access the Internet and the benefits they would gain from getting online. Google is doing its part to educate consumers, and we're also supporting the training of network engineers through organizations such as the African Network Operators' Group and Middle East Network Operators Group.

ITU member countries may cite development benefits as they make proposals for greater centralized control, but new ITU regulations are the wrong solution. We can and should solve problems of access and education without compromising the Internet's essential open and decentralized character.

> *"Internet users, companies, and nations defer to ICANN because . . . to do otherwise hurts no one but yourself. This is a characteristic of a mature global governance organization."*

Existing Institutions Should Be Improved and Continue to Govern the Internet

Jonathan Koppell

Jonathan Koppell is an author, the director of the School of Public Affairs and dean of the College of Public Programs at Arizona State University. In the following viewpoint, he states that the Internet Corporation for Assigned Names and Numbers (ICANN) is the best solution to Internet governance. Although it has been widely criticized by a variety of forces, he maintains that ICANN is still the best option to effectively manage the Internet because it is not threatening to the Internet community, it is responsive yet has a light touch, and it has achieved a stable equilibrium between protecting freedom and regulation. Koppell contends that the predictability and limited scope of ICANN will continue to win out over other Internet governance proposals.

As you read, consider the following questions:

1. According to Koppell, when did the US government create ICANN?

2. What does Koppel cite as ICANN's responsibilities?

3. What did India spearhead in 2011, according to the author?

There's an old saw about the weather: "Everyone complains about it, but no one ever does anything about it." The same might be said about the Internet Corporation for Assigned Names and Numbers, or ICANN.

The U.S. government created ICANN in 1998 to oversee the coordination and management of the Domain Name System, which basically means that it coordinates the unique identifiers of every Web-connected device on the planet. Today, ICANN is most well-known for its rulemaking around website names. For the past 14 years, it has weathered volley after volley of criticisms (not to mention lawsuits) by an eclectic group of individuals, nation states, NGOs [nongovernmental organizations], companies, and global governance bodies for a laundry list of perceived ills, shortcomings, and outright failures. It has been criticized for imposing U.S. values, lacking foresight, and being the catspaw of special interest groups. At the same time, it has been criticized in the halls of the U.S. Congress, its ostensible master, for pursuing paths that were at odds with American interests. It has been taken to task by its own directors, critical of the changing rules by which the organization runs and a lack of transparency in its activities.

Through it all, numerous replacements (often U.N.-affiliated) have been proposed and then fallen. And yet despite the huffing and puffing, ICANN endures.

This presents something of a mystery. Even the most ardent ICANN defender would not argue that this is an organization without fault. Over the years, it has changed course, back-tracked, and pivoted with something less than balletic grace. In fact, the staying power of ICANN offers great insight into the nature of global governance. Its resilience challenges our high-minded assumptions about the importance of "legitimacy." It invites the question: is "democratic governance" really essential for robust international rulemaking?

The Challenges of WCIT-12

The upcoming [December 2012] World Conference on International Telecommunications in Dubai will present another high-profile challenge to ICANN. Leaked proposals for new governance structures and rules have already provoked much discussion and hand-wringing about the dangers of completely revamping the Internet governance architecture. Still, this meeting will almost certainly fail to yield anything like a new blueprint. Why? Because at the end of the day, building and maintaining functional international governance organizations is about keeping key interests satisfied and limiting the scope of authority to matters where those interests agree the existence of global rules is essential. Based on my own examination of global governance organizations in a wide range of substantive arenas, all floated proposals miss this essential reality. ICANN will endure this storm, just as it has so many others, for several reasons.

First, the uncertainty of anything new is highly threatening—to policymakers, business leaders, and government officials. Fears abound that a global Internet regime might usher in an era of greater Internet censorship and control. Of course, this already exists in many countries, but the force of an international rulemaking body could take this beyond the realm of authoritarian regimes. If, for instance, an ICANN successor tried to link domain registration to substantive limitations on content, the effects would not be limited to a single nation. Perhaps even more threatening is the prospect of rules that reshape the business landscape of the Internet. Americans even vaguely familiar with Internet policy know there was a big brouhaha about something called "net neutrality." People got excited enough to stop Congress from altering the competitive landscape—but it turns out other parts of the world have a very different take on the matter. Would a new Internet governor open the door to differential charges for bandwidth use? Certainly a possibility.

In reality, ICANN has a rather light touch. It manages the domain name system—the mechanism by which entering www.slate.com gets you to this website—but leaves many other matters, like access and taxation, alone. As Internet overlords go, it is rather laid back. And it is responsive in a lumbering sort of way. For instance, the recent introduction of multiple language top-level domains finally satisfies one long-standing complaint about the Eurocentrism of Internet governance—even if it took many years to make it happen. The double-whammy of dramatically increased scope along with unpredictable shifts in the internal decision-making process would be too much for the most invested supporters of ICANN to bear.

A Defense of ICANN

Second, flawed though it may be, the ICANN model has achieved a stable equilibrium. In the early days, Internet users around the world had to accept ICANN's rules for a rather practical reason: It, and its antecedent bodies, literally controlled the root servers that function effectively as the switchboard or phonebook of the Internet. You want to be in the phonebook? You accept ICANN's terms. While there are now root servers beyond the reach of the U.S. government (the first ones were all ultimately tied to Uncle Sam), this gatekeeper authority has been replaced by an enormous amount of inertia and acceptance. To those who find ICANN to be undemocratic and unrepresentative of the world's peoples, this might be seen as "authority without legitimacy." Still, it is authority all the same. Many are well-served by ICANN and the rules it promulgates, which vigorously defend intellectual property rights of corporate entities. Other Internet users, companies, and nations defer to ICANN because, well, because everyone else does, and to do otherwise hurts no one but yourself. This is a characteristic of a mature global governance organization. In earlier phases, a similar organization might be required to make more concessions, particularly to key constituencies, as ICANN did, in order to keep them at the table.

Third, ICANN has proven adaptable enough to meet shifting demands and expectations. In my book *World Rule: Accountability, Legitimacy, and the Design of Global Governance*, I argue that global governance operates by a realpolitik that the powerful interests must accept as global governor for it to last. This is necessary but not sufficient. For global governance to matter, everyone else has to go along. And here's the interesting part: The inequity of influence can go only so far. Pushed beyond that point, the disenfranchised *will walk away*. And at that point the value of global regime starts to fade. The balance required is never static. It must be constantly calibrated according to the demands of the moment and the context.

At the ICANN meeting held in Toronto in early October [2012], Fadi Chehadé, in his first meeting as ICANN CEO, intimated that not only is he aware of the criticism of ICANN's decision-making methodology, but that he's also laid out a methodical evolution of the multistakeholder model so desired by ICANN's would-be surrogates. Whether or not that statement will translate to action remains to be seen, but it suggests an awareness of the appeal of some of the movements for democratized Internet governance.

Critics will find the concessions to be too little and too late. But the alternatives are just plain frightening to so many interested parties. Just over a year ago, India spearheaded a proposal to create a *U.N.* Committee for Internet Related Policies [CIRP], which would have had a mandate to "develop and establish international public policies with a view to ensuring coordination and coherence in crosscutting Internetrelated (*sic*) global issues; Coordinate and oversee the bodies responsible for technical and operational functioning of the Internet, including global standards setting; and more. . . ." Even for those dissatisfied with ICANN, this prospect is frightening, because its scope seemed virtually unlimited and procedurally the design contained none of the safeguards against governance run amok that proved crucial in the construction of every effective global governance organization.

Indeed, the reaction to the comprehensive CIRP approach was so tepid that its original sponsor, India, last month declared it had moved away from promoting an ICANN alternative and would instead focus on improving the status quo. ICANN was nimble enough to keep its many constituencies perhaps not happy but not overly unhappy.

Certainly the idea of a multistakeholder governing body sounds like the best way to govern the Internet, an unprecedented technology that connects humanity around the globe, and yet this strange U.S.-dominated entity soldiers on. So it will be after the ITU meeting in Dubai. With the disparate agendas on display in full form, the predictability and limited scope of ICANN will seem awfully acceptable a month from now [December 2012].

> "We ... [need] to listen to the legiti-
> mate concerns expressed by govern-
> ments and work together ... to dem-
> onstrate that the multistakeholder
> model remains the most robust and the
> most effective way to expand the ben-
> efits of the Internet to everyone."

The Internet Should Be Governed by an Inclusive International Alliance

Sally Shipman Wentworth

Sally Shipman Wentworth is the senior manager of public policy for the Internet Society. In the following viewpoint, taken from congressional testimony, she supports a multistakeholder approach to Internet governance but argues that such a strategy will only work if the concerns of developing countries are more effectively addressed. Wentworth suggests that if the Internet community does not do a better job of engaging developing countries and addressing their concerns, these countries will turn to alternative governance strategies—many of which will be detrimental to overall Internet governance. Building bridges to developing countries will provide opportunities for the Internet to grow around the world, Wentworth concludes.

Sally Shipman Wentworth, "Fighting for Internet Freedom," US House of Representatives Energy and Commerce Committee, February 5, 2013.

As you read, consider the following questions:

1. According to Wentworth, how many members does the Internet Society have?

2. How many nations declined to sign the treaty negotiated at the 2012 World Conference on International Telecommunications (WCIT-12), according to the author?

3. What organizations does Wentworth include in the Internet community?

My name is Sally Shipman Wentworth and I am Senior Manager of Public Policy for the Internet Society [ISOC]. The Internet Society is a nonprofit organization dedicated to ensuring the open development, evolution, and use of the Internet for the benefit of all people throughout the world. On behalf of the Internet Society, which is made up of more than 65,000 members and 91 Chapters worldwide, I would like to sincerely thank the leaders of the subcommittees gathered here for the opportunity to testify on the current state of global Internet policy and the future of Internet freedom.

The 2012 WCIT Creates Concerns

Two months ago, in December 2012, the International Telecommunication Union (ITU) convened the World Conference on International Telecommunications (WCIT) in Dubai to review and revise a 1988 treaty called the International Telecommunication Regulations (ITRs). In the months prior to the WCIT, members of the Internet community, advocates, and policymakers began to express concern that some ITU Member States could seek to leverage these telecom treaty negotiations to establish greater governmental control over the Internet. In May 2012, I had the honor of testifying before the Subcommittee on Communications and Technology about WCIT. At the time, we expressed concern that some government proposals would threaten the viability of the successful, existing global multistakeholder model for the Internet, including Internet standards-setting and policy development, and by extension would pose a direct threat to the innovative, collaborative and open nature of the Internet itself.

While the final treaty text was disappointing, it was not as bad as it could have been, thanks in large part to the work of national delegations from the United States, Canada, Australia, Philippines, Kenya and many European Union Member States. However it does contain language that could have a lasting impact on the Internet's infrastructure and operations, and on the content that is so fundamental to its value.

I participated in an Internet Society delegation that attended the Dubai meeting as a Sector Member (i.e., nongovernmental, nonvoting member) of the ITU. As an ITU Sector Member, the Internet Society was able to monitor, but not directly participate in the treaty process, which under ITU rules is the sole province of Member States. As we noted to this committee last May, intergovernmental treaty making processes are not the best way to address critical Internet policy issues because they do not allow for full multistakeholder engagement in the decision making. It is important to point out that the ITU, in response to unprecedented global public interest in the WCIT, took a number of steps to make the process in Dubai more transparent—Sector Members like ISOC participated in preparatory meetings prior to the WCIT, certain sessions at the Conference were webcast and daily updates from Dubai were posted to the ITU website. It will be important for the ITU to build on these steps in the future and to make its processes more transparent and more meaningfully inclusive.

A Failure to Bring Consensus

In the aftermath of WCIT, considerable uncertainty remains as to whether and how the new International Telecommunication Regulations will be implemented and to what extent the lack of consensus will negatively impact global communications networks going forward. We suspect that it will. What *is* certain is that WCIT is one piece of a much longer narrative. At the heart of this narrative is a very basic question over the role of governments in a technology space that is fundamentally borderless. It is a question of how to implement policy—either at the national or international level—in a way that is consistent with a need for global interoperability and accessibility, consensus among all stakeholders, economic growth and on-going innovation. These questions have been around for many years and unsurprisingly, WCIT did not move us toward consensus.

In the end, the results from WCIT are concerning. The lack of consensus among nations and the persistent aims by some governments to establish Internet policy in a closed, intergovernmental context sets the Internet policy dialogue on uncertain footing. It remains to be seen to what extent the highly politicized environment at the WCIT will permeate future Internet governance discussions.

From our perspective, while the WCIT was difficult and presents a host of challenges, it has not shaken our basic confidence that the Internet is fundamentally good for the world and that the multistakeholder model of policy development is still the most effective way to support Internet growth and innovation. We believe that it is our collective responsibility to learn from our experiences in Dubai and work together toward a constructive way forward.

In that light, the Internet Society appreciates the opportunity of this Joint Committee Hearing to examine the potential impact of the WCIT, and seek a path forward that preserves the fundamental values of the open Internet.

A Lack of Consensus Creates New Uncertainty

Although some of the most troubling proposals offered in advance of the WCIT meeting did not make it into the renegotiated treaty, the final document was still controversial enough that 55 nations declined to sign it. The chief question going into WCIT was whether the ITRs would be expanded to apply to international Internet traffic. And while WCIT, as an intergovernmental meeting, could not fully answer that question, certain aspects of the final treaty do anticipate a greater role for the governments and/or the ITU in the Internet. How Member States choose to define that role over the course of the coming years—and to what extent all stakeholders are included in the conversation—will determine how dramatically the ITRs impact the landscape of global Internet policy. If anything, WCIT once again demonstrated the perils of just one stakeholder group—governments—making decisions for all others.

Before highlighting the more concerning aspects of the revised ITRs, it is important to acknowledge the hard work done by so many national delegations to push back on the most prescriptive proposals considered at WCIT. As mentioned above, the U.S. delegation along with delegates from Canada, Sweden, Australia, UK, the Netherlands, Kenya, the Philippines, and many, many others worked tirelessly to oppose the most interventionist proposals offered at the conference. Even in many national delegations that ultimately supported the treaty, Internet advocates toiled against the most prescriptive proposals. Without the engagement of those leaders, including many in Latin America and the Caribbean and also in Africa, the treaty could have been much worse. Importantly, many of these delegations welcomed Internet experts as advisors onto their delegations, a development that we believe was critical to moderating the final treaty text.

As a result of that collective hard work, the final treaty does not directly impose new routing regulations, IP addressing rules, or costly interconnection requirements. It does not endorse a "sender-pays" regime that could have dramatically raised connection costs and barriers to entry, especially for users in the emerging economies. The new treaty also provides for greater transparency regarding mobile roaming rates. At face value, the treaty does not "break" the Internet, and for that, the hundreds of delegates who advocated tirelessly for the Internet's core values should be very proud. At the same time, the Final Acts are ambiguous as to scope and to whom the Regulations will apply so this is an area to watch closely.

A Controversial Internet Resolution

Unfortunately, the WCIT did adopt a controversial new Internet resolution that, in our opinion, suggests a much more prominent role for governments and the ITU on Internet matters, with only a passing reference to the value and promise of multistakeholder policy development. This Resolution selectively quotes from a carefully crafted compromise at the 2005 World Summit on the Information Society [WSIS] which recognized that "the existing arrangements for Internet governance have worked effectively to make the Internet the highly robust, dynamic and geographically diverse medium that it is today, with the private sector taking the lead in day-to-day operations, and with innovation and value creation at the edges." The WCIT Resolution does not reflect the essence of the 2005 WSIS outcome and, in citing the WSIS texts selectively, shifts the emphasis from community and consensus to centralization through government action.

The Internet resolution focuses on the very heart of the longstanding debate between those who envision a more direct role for intergovernmental organizations in the management of Internet communication, and those who support the existing, open, multistakeholder model of Internet governance. That model, which is unique to the Internet, engages technologists, the private sector and civil society in a bottom-up, consensus driven approach to standards setting, Internet development, and management. This approach has proven to be nimble and effective in ensuring the stability, security, and availability of the global infrastructure, while still giving sovereign nations the flexibility to develop Internet policies within their borders. And while UN members formally endorsed the multistakeholder model in 2005, a strong undercurrent of support for greater governmental involvement has remained among some countries. In fact, these countries see the UN as the natural home for intergovernmental cooperation and believe that the ITU, as the UN specialized agency for telecommunication, is the "logical organization" to deal with Internet issues. At WCIT, that view held greater sway for some countries than ever before.

In addition to the broad Internet resolution, the treaty also contains new language relating to network security and unsolicited bulk electronic communications ("spam"). While the language for both of those provisions is quite general, there is concern that government implementation of these provisions will ultimately place restrictions or limitations on the Internet and the content it carries.

Looking ahead, the question now for all of us is how to translate the WCIT experience into tangible actions and more widespread buy-in for the Internet's multistakeholder model of Internet policy development. We need to take the lessons learned seriously or we will continue to be faced with the kinds of divisions that resurfaced at the WCIT.

Global Tensions

While WCIT outcomes remain ambiguous, the Conference did crystallize deep tensions that may be poised to define Internet policymaking at the global level. The tensions that led to the WCIT outcome are not new—many of the same issues that colored the debate in Dubai also factored heavily at the World Summit on the Information Society (WSIS) in 2003 and 2005 and at subsequent international meetings. How we collectively respond to WCIT, will determine if those divisions deepen rather than diminish.

In some ways, the debate at WCIT helped to clarify the risk: that the global Internet may give way to a set of national Internets, each with its own rules and gatekeepers, and with higher costs for all. If that happens, the platform will become more fragmented and fewer people will benefit from it. From our perspective as an organization that believes that the Internet becomes more valuable and powerful as it becomes more globally diverse, this is an outcome that must be averted.

WCIT provided a great deal of insight into developing country priorities with respect to the Internet. They have important questions and, in many cases, legitimate concerns. They have concerns about the high cost of connectivity, privacy, and consumer protection. They have a desire for more information in the areas of IP addressing and numbering. They have a desire to drive more local traffic and content. These countries aim to make smart infrastructure investments, to get answers to weighty questions surrounding censorship and human rights, and to have their experts represented in technical standards–setting bodies and international policy processes.

If we do not increase our efforts to address these issues, there is a risk that many countries will turn to sources that do not support the Internet's multistakeholder model. In discussions with our members and partners from across the global Internet community, including individual users, industry, engineers, and civil society groups and government representatives, the consensus is clearly in favor of more problem solving and more capacity building. In short, more engagement, not less, is the answer.

Engagement Is Key

This emphasis on engagement becomes more important as we look at the timeline for upcoming international meetings thru 2015 where we could see continued efforts to undermine the multistakeholder approach. In 2013, the ITU will host the

World Telecommunication/ICT Policy Forum followed by the ITU's Plenipotentiary Conference in Busan, South Korea in October 2014, which will set the scope and strategic vision for the ITU and another international treaty. We fully expect that the role of the ITU in Internet policy issues will figure prominently in the political debate at the Plenipotentiary Conference. Between now and then, a series of important regional and global ITU development meetings will set the regional framework for the negotiations in Busan. On a positive note, meetings of the Internet Governance Forum (IGF) in 2013 and 2014 offer a non-negotiating forum in which more productive dialogue can take place and, as I outline below, present an opportunity to tangibly support the multistakeholder approach.

At the Internet Society, we recognize that certain geopolitical and substantive rifts among countries are not likely to be solved before 2014. However, we can work with those countries that want to engage to take those core elements of an open Internet model and apply that approach to address the problems that policy makers face all over the world.

Thus, in addition to presenting significant challenges, WCIT should be a call to action for members of the global Internet community—including technologists, policymakers, advocates, industry leaders, and individual users—to focus their efforts to improve and expand the multistakeholder model of Internet governance so that it continues to serve the needs of *all* users across the globe.

Staying Engaged and Building Bridges

Although WCIT revealed deep regional and national differences over policy, there were bright spots to recognize as well. In fact, in reading through the final statements by governments to the conference, we see a number of strong statements of support for the overall Internet model, even among those who chose to sign the treaty. Many countries stated

The Internet Ecosystem

Internet Ecosystem is the term used to describe the organizations and communities that help the Internet work and evolve. . . .

Organizations that make up the Internet Ecosystem include:

- Technologists, engineers, architects, creatives, organizations such as the Internet Engineering Task Force (IETF) and the World Wide Web Consortium (W3C) who help coordinate and implement open standards.

- Global and local Organizations that manage resources for global addressing capabilities such as the Internet Corporation for Assigned Names and Numbers (ICANN), including its operation of the Internet Assigned Numbers Authority (IANA) function, Regional Internet Registries (RIR), and Domain Name Registries and Registrars.

- Operators, engineers, and vendors that provide network infrastructure services such as Domain Name Service (DNS) providers, network operators, and Internet Exchange Points (IXPs)

- Internet Users who use the Internet to communicate with each other and offer services

- Educators that teach others and build capacity for developing and using Internet technologies. . .

- Policy and Decision Makers that provide local and global policy development and governance.

Internet Society, "Who Owns the Internet?,"
October 2010. www.internetsociety.org.

their commitment to playing an active role in the Internet economy, and to ensuring that their citizens are able to take advantage of the full value that the Internet has to offer. This is something to build upon. Our challenge, and the challenge of all supporters of the multistakeholder approach, is not only to advocate for the model, but also to ensure that it actually works for those who may doubt its effectiveness.

We can look to the Internet Governance Forum as a constructive mechanism within the UN system to bring together Internet stakeholders from around the world and as a model for multistakeholder dialogue that is inclusive of governments but not centrally managed by governments. The Internet Society has been a long-standing supporter of the IGF model, believing that genuine progress can be made in this environment. The vision of the IGF is also taking hold at the regional and national levels. In 2012, we participated in African, Arab, Caribbean, Latin American, and Indian IGF meetings. In the U.S., IGF-USA has become a very useful and important national event. But the IGF is only possible with the sustained support and commitment by all.

Beyond the dialogue, tangible action is also needed. The Internet community, through organizations like the Regional Internet Registries (RIRs), the Internet Corporation for Assigned Names and Numbers (ICANN), the Internet Engineering Task Force (IETF), the Internet Society (ISOC) and many others, has a long track record of working hard to make the Internet more inclusive and better for everyone through concrete activities. Dating back to the earliest days of the Internet's development, there was a keen recognition that, to be truly successful, the Internet needed advocates around the world that could sustain and build Internet infrastructure and, in doing so, would expand the Internet to their local communities—whether in Silicon Valley or at a local university in Kenya. Beginning in 1992, the Internet Society hosted frequent developing country workshops that were attended by over

1,300 participants from over 94 countries. Many of the workshop participants are now Internet leaders in their country or region. We know that some of this training supported Internet pioneers in Ghana, Thailand, Argentina, and Brazil who are now spearheading Internet connectivity growth and sustainable Internet human capacity development and training in their communities. We continue this work today, strengthening partnerships and opportunities for the Internet to grow around the world.

Future Commitment Is Needed

The Internet Society is deeply grateful to the members of the subcommittees that called this hearing for addressing an issue of vital importance to the global Internet. We also sincerely appreciate the longstanding commitment of the United States government to the multistakeholder model of the Internet.

I want to leave the Subcommittees with one key message: please continue your support for the multistakeholder model of Internet policy development, both at home and abroad. As we face a high level of uncertainty going forward, the best way to respond post-WCIT is to listen to the legitimate concerns expressed by governments and work together to engage appropriately to demonstrate that the multistakeholder model remains the most robust and the most effective way to expand the benefits of the Internet to everyone. The importance of sustained U.S. commitment to the principles of the global, open Internet cannot be overstated. While the impact of WCIT will be felt for years to come, we can work together to ensure the Internet continues to transcend political divides, and serves as an engine for human empowerment throughout the world.

Periodical and Internet Sources Bibliography

The following articles have been selected to supplement the diverse views presented in this chapter.

Jermyn Brooks   "Hands Off the Internet!," *New York Times*, December 6, 2012.

Vinton Cerf   "'Father of the Internet': Why We Must Fight for Its Freedom," CNN.com, November 30, 2012. www.cnn.com.

Dan Gillmor   "UN Regulation Talks in Dubai Threaten Internet Freedom," *The Guardian* (Manchester, UK), December 4, 2012.

Karl Grossman   "Will the Internet Remain Free?," *Huffington Post*, January 29, 2013. www.huffingtonpost .com.

Timothy B. Lee   "Why the ITU Is the Wrong Place to Set Internet Standards," Ars Technica, December 13, 2012. http://arstechnica.com.

Dick Morris   "Stop UN Regulation of the Internet," *The Hill*, October 10, 2012.

Milton Mueller   "ITU Phobia: Why WCIT Was Derailed," Internet Governance Project, December 18, 2012. www.internetgovernance.org.

Stewart M. Patrick   "UN Control of the Internet? An Idea Whose Time Will Never Come," Council on Foreign Relations, December 4, 2012. www.cfr.org.

Brett D. Schaefer and James L. Gattuso   "Knowing When to Walk Away: The UN and Internet Freedom," Heritage Foundation, November 29, 2012. www.heritage.org.

Hamadoun I. Touré   "UN: We Seek to Bring Internet to All," *Wired*, November 7, 2012.

What Are the Best Ways to Fight Internet Censorship?

Chapter Preface

In May 2011, a federal lawsuit was filed in US District Court for the Northern District of California against Cisco Systems, a multinational corporation based in the United States that designs and manufactures networking equipment for the Internet. The lawsuit was filed by the Human Rights Law Foundation on behalf of members of the Falun Gong, a spiritual and philosophical movement based in China. The lawsuit alleges that Cisco customized and sold its web-filtering software to help the Chinese government identify and track Falun Gong members, which led to multiple arrests of group members, imprisonment, forced labor, torture, and even death.

Falun Gong is a spiritual movement that originated in China in 1992. Combining the practice of meditation, qigong exercises, and a moral philosophy centered around the three tenets of truthfulness, forbearance, and compassion, Falun Gong quickly gained supporters. It is estimated that by 2000, there were several million members of the movement in China.

This growing popularity of Falun Gong worried Chinese government officials. Although the government had initially tolerated—and even supported—Falun Gong, the group's impressive size and potential social and political power led officials to crack down on the movement in 1999. It designated Falun Gong a "heretical" organization and began to block Internet access to any website that offered information about the group or even discussed the controversy surrounding it. Falun Gong members lost their jobs, were arrested and imprisoned in remote labor camps. Human rights organizations have documented cases of members who were subjected to harsh psychiatric abuse meant to "reeducate" members into renouncing the Falun Gong. Other members just disappeared or were brutally beaten to death. Yet despite the Chinese government's repression, millions of Falun Gong members in China continued to practice in secret.

In the late 1990s, Chinese officials began to design and develop technology to flush out, identify, and monitor members of the group as they communicated online. Known as the Great Firewall of China, the result was a massive censorship and surveillance program that employed multiple content-filtering techniques to tightly control the Internet and monitor any user that officials suspected was a threat to the state. These threats included the Falun Gong and other religious groups, pro-democracy and other political activists, and supporters of the Dalai Lama and Tibetan independence.

Despite the nefarious aims of the Great Firewall of China, many businesses saw the immense program as an economic opportunity. One of these companies was Cisco Systems. It is alleged that Cisco was strategizing as early as 2002 to market its technology to China and to help develop censorship and surveillance systems that would inevitably result in the oppression of political dissidents and others. Reports have surfaced that internal Cisco documents reveal that engineers at the company were clearly aware that the technology would be used against the Falun Gong.

Cisco's marketing strategy worked: they sold more than one hundred thousand dollars worth of routers and switches to the Chinese government as part of the Great Firewall of China. However, Cisco officials deny that the company customized its technology to fit government surveillance and censorship requirements, nor did it help design the firewall system. Critics charge that the evidence shows that the company did both.

When Cisco's role in the Great Firewall of China was revealed in 2004, it sparked a debate on the double-edged role that American Internet technology plays on the global landscape. US government officials quickly called for investigations on the Cisco controversy, outraged that a US technology company would facilitate Internet censorship and the repression of millions of people. Arvind Ganesan, a director at Human Rights Watch, suggested that companies should refrain from doing business with repressive countries like China. "If you know ahead of time that a sale could lead to human rights violations, and there's no way of mitigating that, maybe you shouldn't offer it to that entity," he stated regarding the Cisco lawsuit.

The Cisco incident opened a dialogue on US corporate responsibility, Internet censorship and surveillance, Internet freedom, and human rights. It is also one of the subjects discussed in the following chapter, which debates the most effective ways to fight Internet censorship.

"It is time for the State Department to end the empty promises and . . . act in defense of global Internet freedom."

A More Proactive Defense of Internet Freedom Will Reduce Censorship

Helle C. Dale and Jessica Zuckerman

Helle C. Dale is the senior fellow for public diplomacy and Jessica Zuckerman is a research assistant at the Heritage Foundation, a conservative Washington, DC, think tank. In the following viewpoint, they suggest that the US government, particularly the State Department, needs to significantly improve efforts to defend Internet speech. One key improvement, they argue, would be to ensure that funding moves more efficiently and quickly to organizations that are pursuing Internet freedom. Dale and Zuckerman urge the US government to clearly call out countries that are the worst perpetrators of Internet censorship. To that end, they contend, a global coalition should be organized to advocate for the protection of freedom of expression on the Internet.

As you read, consider the following questions:

1. According to a 2011 Freedom House report cited by the authors, what countries are at the top of the list of the worst Internet censors?

2. According to a recent OpenNet Initiative report, cited by Dale and Zuckerman, what big Internet security companies have sold their web filtering systems to repressive regimes?

3. How much funding do the authors say was allocated by the Broadcasting Board of Governors (BBG) for a grant to the Global Internet Freedom Consortium?

More than 2 billion people worldwide now have some degree of access to the Internet, a figure that has doubled over the past five years. Yet while the Internet is emerging as an increasingly powerful tool for political activism, governments around the world are also becoming more expert at controlling electronic communication.

As part of the U.S. effort to defend freedom of speech and expression throughout the globe, Secretary of State Hillary Clinton has asserted the Administration's dedication to Internet freedom time and time again. Actions, however, speak louder than words.

U.S. Agencies and Appropriations

It took the State Department more than three years to allocate the $50 million given to the department by Congress for its global Internet freedom efforts. In this year's [2011's] Continuing Resolution, Congress gave another $20 million to the State Department and $10 million to the Broadcasting Board of Governors (BBG) to further pursue their Internet freedom agendas. This time around, the funding must move more speedily and efficiently to invest in proven technologies and fill gaps in private sector investment. At the same time, the

U.S. government should call attention to those countries that are the worst perpetrators of Internet censorship. These offenses are already recorded in the State Department's Annual Human Rights Report to Congress.

Internet Freedom's Worst Offenders

In January, Freedom House released "Freedom on the Net 2011: A Global Assessment of the Internet and Digital Media," examining Internet freedom in 37 countries across the globe. Most of the worst offenders are no surprise. At the top of the list were: Iran, Burma, Cuba, China, Tunisia, Vietnam, Saudi Arabia, Ethiopia, Belarus, Bahrain, and Thailand.

The report shows that threats to Internet freedom continue to grow. In 19 of the 37 countries examined, the Internet was subject to some degree of centralized control. In Egypt, for example, the decision of the government to completely shut down the Internet for five days in the midst of political upheaval and protests this past January showed the power of such centralized control.

Further, in 12 out of the 37 countries examined, officials imposed repeated blocks or bans on popular social networking and media sharing sites, such as Facebook, Twitter, and YouTube. Bloggers and other Internet users were arrested in 23 of the 27 nations, while activists' networks were targeted or under surveillance in at least 12 countries.

Freedom House is not the only one tracking the perpetrators of cyber repression. Each year on World Day Against Cybercensorship, March 12, Reporters without Borders publishes its own list of "Internet enemies." Citing many of the same top offenders, this year Reporters without Borders highlighted the oppressive cyber policies of Burma, China, Cuba, Iran, North Korea, Saudi Arabia, Syria, Turkmenistan, Uzbekistan, and Vietnam. As of March of this year, these countries had some 119 netizens behind bars—China, Vietnam, and Iran being the worst offenders.

Corporate Responsibility

Disconcertingly, the mass Web filtering tools used by Middle Eastern and North African governments are often created by Western companies. According to a recent report by the Open-Net Initiative, a collaborative effort between several universities dedicated to exposing and analyzing Internet filtering operations, McAfee, Websense, Blue Coat Systems, Palo Alto Networks, and Netsweeper have all sold their Web filtering systems to repressive regimes that use these products to censor Web content. Websense has publicized a clear policy that it "does not sell to governments or Internet Service Providers (ISPs) that are engaged in government imposed censorship," but it has sold a product to Yemen that filters content and also prevents users from disguising their identity from monitors.

In defense of their actions, these companies argue that they have no control over how clients use their products, just as a car company does not have responsibility for how people operate its vehicles. While at some level this argument seems reasonable, it does not account for the fact that many of these companies have not only provided the regimes with the requisite software, but also continually update the list of URLs that are filtered through the program. This updating has an immediate effect on the information that entire nations of people can access.

The State Department's Actions

In February [2011], Secretary of State Hillary Clinton reasserted the Department of State's dedication to Internet freedom, committing to "a comprehensive and innovative approach—one that matches our diplomacy with our technology, secure distribution networks for tools and direct support for those on the front lines." The actions of the department, however, have not fully matched this commitment.

While the State Department dragged its feet on doling out its funding, the Broadcasting Board of Governors (BBG) stepped up. With its modest amount of funding—$1.5 million—the BBG gave a grant to the Global Internet Freedom Consortium, run by the Chinese exiled Falun Gong religious sect, specializing in developing and deploying anti-censorship technologies. The Global Internet Freedom Consortium supports the proliferation of the anti-censorship programs Ultrareach and Freegate, just two of the proven circumvention technologies on the market.

Within the Department of State, however, $28 million of the total $50 million received by the State Department for promoting Internet freedom remained unallocated until May of this year. Noting this fact, Congress gave the department only $20 million in fiscal year 2011 and gave the BBG another $10 million. State has since announced its plans to allocate the funds "like venture capitalists," offering grants to fund the further development of circumvention technologies and to help train activists fighting cyber repression across the globe. Congress should continue to hold State to this commitment.

Further U.S. Action Is Needed

The Administration should:

- *Spend Internet freedom funds wisely.* Funds to support Internet freedom ought to be efficiently directed toward providing an incentive for private companies to design more effective firewall circumvention technologies. The BBG has enjoyed a degree of success in funding the Global Internet Freedom Consortium.

- *Speak out against Internet freedom's worst offenders.* The U.S. should continue to unequivocally condemn nations who jail citizens for communicating on the net. Offenses can be recorded in the Annual Human Rights Report. The U.S. should let every nation know that its status as a free nation depends not only on its human rights record but also on the degree to which it restricts freedom of expression over the Web.

- *Encourage other nations to join a coalition*, which could provide the venue for "naming and shaming" offenders. The Financial Action Task Force (FATF) provides a model for voluntary inter-governmental cooperation. Its purpose is combating money laundering and terrorist financing, and it encourages the development of national and international policies in member nations. An international Internet Freedom Task Force could similarly encourage the protection of freedom of expression on the Internet.

It is time for the State Department to end the empty promises and stop hoarding scarce funds. The U.S. must act in defense of global Internet freedom.

"*Internet firms will never please every-one. But good laws at least point them in the right direction.*"

Internet Freedom: Free to Choose

The Economist

The Economist is a weekly news and international affairs publication originating in Great Britain. In the following viewpoint, the growing debate over how companies should respond to nations that want to constrain free speech online is explored. For many free speech advocates, web companies have gone too far in responding to concerns over nudity, controversial speech and videos, and copyright issues, according to the author. There is a growing consensus that smart legislation could help Internet companies avoid bad decisions, such as strict or costly libel laws. Such laws, The Economist contends, can reassure parents and satisfy security concerns without being absurd and overzealous in practice. Web services are working to find that difficult balance and are exploring ways to appeal to consumers, the author concludes. ·

As you read, consider the following questions:

1. According to Google statistics cited by the author, how many countries had asked to block content in the last six months of 2011?

2. When was the Global Network Initiative founded, according to *The Economist*?

3. What sentence does the author say an Italian court handed down in 2010 to three Google executives after a video showing the bullying of a disabled boy appeared on YouTube?

The arrest of a senior executive rarely brings helpful headlines. But when Brazilian authorities briefly detained Google's country boss on September 26th—for refusing to remove videos from its YouTube subsidiary that appeared to breach electoral laws—they helped the firm repair its image as a defender of free speech.

Two weeks earlier those credentials looked tarnished. Google blocked net users in eight countries from viewing a film trailer that had incensed Muslims. In six states, including India and Saudi Arabia, local courts banned the footage. In Egypt and Libya, where protesters attacked American embassies and killed several people, Google took the video down of its own accord.

The row sparked concern about how internet firms manage public debate and how companies based in countries that cherish free speech should respond to states that want to constrain it. (Freedom House, a campaigning think-tank, reckons that restrictions on the internet are increasing in 20 of the 47 states it surveys.)

In June Google revealed that 45 countries had asked it to block content in the last six months of 2011. Some requests were easily rejected. Officials in the Canadian passport office

Censorship and the Global Online Freedom Act

In recent decades the Internet spreads information rapidly throughout the world and has frequently been targeted for government censorship. The Communist Party of China (CPC), which has ruled China since 1949, is heavy-handed when it comes to Internet censorship. Under the CPC's governance, websites like GoogleEarth and the BBC have been blocked or restricted. According to a Harvard study, there are over 18,000 websites blocked from within the country. China's Internet censorship policy is labeled "Pervasive" by the OpenNet Initiative (a global project that monitors and reports on Internet censorship and the surveillance practices of nations around the world)—the worst ranking a country can receive. Besides the Internet, the CPC censors the news media, television, radio, film, and even video games.

In the U.S., the proposed Global Online Freedom Act will hold U.S.-based companies liable for helping government officials in other countries censor the Internet. The proposed Act will also bar U.S. companies from disclosing personally identifiable information about any Internet user. The Global Online Freedom Act, if passed, could help to combat some of the Internet censorship that is taking place all over the globe.

Global Issues in Context, *"Censorship,"* 2013.
www.gale.cengage.com.

asked it to block a video advocating independence for Quebec, in which a citizen urinated on his passport and flushed it down the toilet.

Most firms do accept that they must follow the laws of countries in which they operate (Nazi content is banned in

Germany, for example). Big internet firms can prevent users accessing content their governments consider illegal, while leaving it available to visitors from countries where no prohibition applies. Some pledge to be transparent about their actions—Twitter, like Google, releases six-monthly reports of government requests to block information. It also alerts citizens when it has censored content in their country.

Legislators in America want more firms to follow suit. In March a congressional subcommittee approved the latest revision of the Global Online Freedom Act, first drafted in 2004. This would require technology firms operating in a designated group of restrictive countries to publish annual reports showing how they deal with human-rights issues. It would waive this for firms that sign up to non-governmental associations that provide similar oversight, such as the Global Network Initiative. Founded in 2008 by Google, Microsoft, Yahoo! and a coalition of human-rights groups, it has since stalled. Facebook joined in May but only as an observer. Twitter is absent, too.

Managing free speech in home markets is hard, too. American websites enjoy broad freedom but most users support policies that forbid hate speech or obscenity, even when these are not illegal. Well-drafted community guidelines give platforms personality (and reassure nervous parents). But overzealous moderation can have "absurd and censorious" results, says Kevin Bankston at the Centre for Democracy and Technology, a think-tank. Citing rules that prohibit sexually loaded content, Facebook last month removed a *New Yorker* cartoon that depicted a bare-chested Eve in the Garden of Eden. It also routinely removes its users' photos of breast-feeding if they show the mother's nipples, however unsalacious the picture may be.

Commercial concerns can trump consistency. In July Twitter briefly suspended the account of a journalist who had published the e-mail address of a manager at NBC while criticising it for lacklustre coverage of the London Olympics. Twitter admitted it had monitored tweets that criticised the firm (a business partner) and vowed not to do so again. Automated systems can also be too zealous. Citing a copyright violation, YouTube's robots briefly blocked a video of Michelle Obama speaking at the Democratic Party convention on September 4th (perhaps because of background music). In August official footage of NASA's Mars landing suffered the same fate. Jillian York at the Electronic Frontier Foundation, a free-speech group, thinks some services refuse to host any images of nudes, however innocent or artistic, because they can trigger anti-porn software.

Aware of the problem, web firms are trying to improve their systems. Facebook's reporting tool now helps users resolve simple grievances among themselves. Tim Wu at Columbia Law School speculates that video-hosting services may one day ask committees of users to decide whether to allow sensitive footage to be shown in their countries. Europeans unvexed by nudity might then escape American advertisers' prudish standards. But it would be hard to enforce on social networks that prize their cross-border ties.

Simpler remedies might make users happier. Rebecca MacKinnon, an expert on internet freedom, says web firms act as "legislature, police, judge, jury and executioner" in enforcing moderation policies and should offer their members more opportunity to appeal. Marietje Schaake, a Dutch politician helping to formulate European digital policy, thinks web users wanting to challenge egregious judgments need more help from the law.

Changing the law in some countries could help platforms avoid bad decisions. Some governments menace web firms with antiquated media laws that consider them publishers, not just hosts, of their users' content. In 2010 an Italian court handed down suspended jail sentences to three Google executives after a video showing the bullying of a disabled boy appeared on YouTube—even though the firm removed it when notified.

Sites in countries with fierce or costly libel laws often censor content the moment they receive a complaint, regardless of its merit. England (Scotland's legal system is different) is changing the law to grant greater immunity to internet platforms that give complainants easy access to content originators.

Some users value avoiding offence more highly than the risk of censorship. The majority see things the other way round. So internet firms will never please everyone. But good laws at least point them in the right direction.

"Fighting [Internet] censors every step of the way is an army of self-described 'hacktivists.'"

Cracking the "Great Firewall" of China's Web Censorship

Paul Wiseman

Paul Wiseman is a reporter for USA Today. *In the following viewpoint, he contends that hacktivists (computer hackers who hack to achieve political goals) are essential in the fight against state-imposed Internet censorship. Hacktivism, Wiseman asserts, has been particularly effective in helping Chinese citizens access information on subjects banned by Chinese censors, such as Tibetan independence or China's human rights record. The Chinese employ a variety of methods to suppress information, but Wiseman illustrates, savvy netizens and hacktivists can find a way around even advanced censorship software and practices. Wiseman reports that hacktivists work hard to stay abreast of Chinese tricks and techniques as well as technological advances in censorship and surveillance software.*

As you read, consider the following questions:

1. According to Wiseman, how many Internet users were there in China by the end of March 2008?

2. What does Wiseman report happened to the Internet portal Sina after it altered a newspaper headline in China?

3. What is the significance of the Chinese term for "harmonized" among Chinese internet users, according to the author?

If an Internet user in China searches for the word "persecution," he or she is likely to come up with a link to a blank screen that says "page cannot be displayed."

The same is true of searches for "Tibetan independence," "democracy movements" or stranger sounding terms such as "oriental red space time"—code for an anti-censorship video made secretly by reporters at China's state TV station.

It's a reflection of the stifling, bizarre and sometimes dangerous world of Internet censorship in China. The communist government in Beijing is intensifying its efforts to control what its citizens can read and discuss online as political tensions rise ahead of this summer's Olympic Games [in 2008].

The Battle Lines Are Drawn

Fighting the censors every step of the way is an army of self-described "hacktivists" such as Bill Xia, a Chinese-born software engineer who lives in North Carolina. Xia and others are engaged in a kind of technological arms race, inventing software and using other tactics to allow ordinary Chinese to beat the "Great Firewall of China" and access information on sensitive subjects such as Chinese human rights and Tibet, the province where pro-independence sentiment has boiled over in recent months.

Invoking the hit science-fiction movie *The Matrix*, Xia has compared what he does to giving Chinese Web surfers a "red pill" that lets them see reality for the first time. He spends long nights struggling to outfox an opponent—the Chinese government—that is arguably the world's best at controlling what its people see.

"They are very smart," Xia says. "We have to move very quickly."

To Americans and other Westerners, it might seem odd that Internet censorship is still possible at a time when You-Tube, satellite TV and online chat rooms produce an overwhelming flow of real-time news and data. Yet authoritarian regimes from Cuba to Saudi Arabia to Pakistan rely on a mix of sophisticated technology and old-fashioned intimidation to ensure that dissent can be repressed, even in the Information Age.

China: King of Internet Censorship

No one does it quite like China, which has proved that old-school communist apparatchiks [bureaucrats] could tame something as wild as the Web. China has the world's "most sophisticated" Internet filtering system, according to the Open-Net Initiative, an academic cooperative that tracks censorship issues.

At the heart of China's censorship efforts is a delicate balancing act.

Unlike communist North Korea, which bans online access to its general population, China is encouraging Internet usage as it rushes to construct a modern economy. This year [2008], the number of Internet users in China surpassed the USA for the first time, hitting 233 million by the end of March. However, China's government does not tolerate opposition and is wary of the variety of views and information the Web brings.

Last month's [March 2008] pro-independence riots in Tibet, and the accompanying furor that followed the international relay of the Olympic torch, have led Chinese officials to step up their Web censorship. News articles and video clips concerning Tibet were banned for several days. Xia expects the censorship will tighten further in the coming months because "many human rights organizations will be trying to get their voices heard" during the Olympic Games.

"There will be lots of news out there," says Xia, who admits he had little interest in politics until the Chinese government banned the spiritual group Falun Gong in 1999 and started persecuting its members. Xia is a member of the group.

"Lots of unexpected things are going to happen," he says.

Forbidden Words and Stories

The most basic tool at the Chinese government's disposal— and, perhaps, the one most easily circumvented by dissidents—is to ban access within China to websites such as Voice of America or to certain stories that contain sensitive words and phrases. For example, several recent *USA Today* stories about Tibet are currently blocked within China.

Other censorship methods are more blunt. This month [April 2008], Hu Jia, an activist on AIDS and other issues, was sentenced to 3½ years in jail for articles he wrote for Boxun-.com, a U.S.-based Chinese-language website that is banned in China. At least 48 cyberdissidents are behind bars in China, according to Reporters Without Borders.

Chinese officials with the Ministry of Information Industry, the State Council Information Office and other agencies declined to comment on why China restricts content on the Internet.

Past explanations by the government focus on the need to prevent "harmful" content such as pornography and terrorism from reaching citizens.

Even those "hacktivists" who live outside the country apparently face risks. Peter Li—a Chinese-born, Princeton-educated computer specialist—says he learned that two years ago when he answered the doorbell at his home in suburban Atlanta.

Three men burst inside, beat him, bound him and gagged him with duct tape, he says. Speaking Korean and Chinese, they ransacked his filing cabinets and hauled off his two computers. They ignored a TV, a camcorder and other valuables.

The FBI and the local Fulton County, Ga., police still have not found the men responsible for the attack. But Li, who like Xia is a practicing member of Falun Gong, says it was an attempt by the Chinese government to shut him up.

"I know it wasn't a simple robbery," he says.

The Chinese government has denied any involvement in the raid on Li's home.

How China Does It

There are a range of other methods China has used to suppress information. Among them:

Creating bottlenecks. In *The Atlantic* magazine last month, journalist James Fallows noted that Internet traffic to China is channeled through three computer centers—near Beijing, Shanghai and the southern city of Guangzhou.

In the USA, by contrast, the Internet is designed to avoid traffic jams by allowing information to flow from as many sources as possible. By building in chokepoints, Fallows wrote, "Chinese authorities can easily do something that would be harder in most developed countries: physically monitor all traffic into or out of the country."

Checking Internet traffic for subversive material. This is done in much the same way police dogs sniff airport luggage for illegal drugs. The Chinese install "packet sniffers" and special routers to inspect data as they cruise past the chokepoints. If the detectors spot a Chinese Internet user trying to visit a suspect website—say, one run by Falun Gong—they can block the connection.

What Is Online Activism?

Online activism is the use of digital tools or electronic communication technologies to facilitate communication and coordination among activists, advocates, their supporters, and the media. Online activism campaigns are most often centered on issues, but also arise in the form of citizen journalism to disseminate news about current events. Tools of online activism include the World Wide Web, social media networks, texting, email, listservs, digital video, podcasts, blogs, and online petitions and fundraising campaigns. International human rights groups, nongovernmental organizations (NGOs), political organizations, non-traditional media organizations and citizen journalists, environmental groups, and citizen movements commonly incorporate at least one form of online activism into their operations.

In 2011, approximately 2.3 billion people worldwide regularly used the Internet. World mobile phone (cell phone) subscriptions reached 5.6 billion—more than 75 percent of the world's population—according to the International Telecommunication Union. The number of people worldwide who used any form of electronic communication at least once per week tripled between 2003 and 2009. The proliferation of access to the Internet and other communication technologies allowed advocacy groups to share information, especially in and from remote areas. Online activism also became an easy and cost-effective method to disseminate information in parts of the world with government-controlled traditional media.

Global Issues in Context, *"Online Activism,"* 2013.
www.gale.cengage.com.

A frustrated user might get a message saying: "Site not found." Similarly, Web users can be stopped from leaving subversive comments in online forums. Sometimes they get notes back warning them to behave or apologizing for technical problems.

Demanding self-censorship. Chinese authorities hold commercial websites responsible for what appears on them. In Beijing—where Internet controls are strictest—authorities issue orders to website managers through cellphone text messages and demand that they comply within 30 minutes, according to a report last fall by Reporters Without Borders.

When the Internet portal Sina altered the headline of a state media report on the economy, the government accused it of "inciting violence" and excluded it from interviews with important officials for a month. The website NetEase fired two editors after they published a 2006 poll showing that 64% of 10,000 participants would not want to be reborn as Chinese.

Issuing propaganda. Authorities in the southern boomtown of Shenzhen created two cute cartoon cybercops—the male Jingjing and the female Chacha—that pop up on websites to remind Internet users they're being watched. The *Beijing Youth Daily* newspaper quoted a security official admitting that the big-eyed cartoon duo were designed "to intimidate."

Chinese officials also order websites to reprint official propaganda such as a report encouraging Internet users to abide by online etiquette.

Getting outside help. China has policed the Internet with assistance from U.S. firms. Cisco Systems, for instance, supplied the original routers China used to monitor Internet traffic. (Cisco has said it didn't tailor its equipment for the Chinese market.)

Google created a censored search engine for China. Outside China, users who search Google Images for "Tiananmen Square" get pictures from the 1989 pro-democracy protests that ended in a crackdown that left hundreds dead—and included the iconic photograph of a lone man staring down a line of Chinese tanks. Inside China, users get only tourist images of Tiananmen Square and the Forbidden City across the street.

Yahoo turned over e-mail that authorities used to jail a Chinese journalist who leaked information about China's attempts to censor coverage of the anniversary of the Tiananmen crackdown. (The companies say they had to comply with Chinese law.)

Despite China's strategies, sophisticated Internet users in the country "can pretty much get as much information as (they) want," says Jeremy Goldkom, the Beijing-based editor of the China media website danwei.org. "But what (the government does) is make it difficult, so the ordinary person is not going to bother."

Censorship Loopholes

In 2002, Xia formed a company—Dynamic Internet Technology—to wage cyberwar on the Chinese regime. He created Freegate, a software program that finds holes in the firewall and takes Chinese Internet users to banned websites, undetected.

Xia also sends millions of e-mail messages into China for customers such as Voice of America and the activist group Human Rights in China. The e-mails contain links to forbidden sites at an ever-changing list of temporary Internet addresses, part of an effort to stay a step ahead of Chinese censors.

Traffic on his network of "proxy" websites picked up in February, when heavy snows blocked traffic and shut train service in southern China, Xia says.

The Chinese government was reluctant to admit anything had gone wrong, so frustrated travelers turned to renegade websites to get practical information on weather conditions and rail service.

Even so, Chinese authorities constantly are finding new ways to plug the holes Freegate finds or to otherwise stymie Xia's efforts. He figures he has upgraded Freegate 20 times. "We're gradually getting faster and faster" at fixing problems with the software when Chinese users report them, he says.

Chinese Internet users also use decidedly low-tech methods to evade official attempts to censor their e-mail or online commentary.

They will, for instance, try to throw off the cybercops by inserting spaces or punctuation marks between characters—much as spammers in the USA try to beat e-mail filters by offering "Free Vi@gra!"

The authorities try to update their list of banned terms—now running into the hundreds—to include those with creative punctuation.

Rebecca MacKinnon, former Beijing bureau chief for CNN, spotted the way some cheeky Chinese Internet users stayed ahead of the censors. Whenever their edgy comments were purged from a website, they'd joke online that they'd "been harmonized"—a sarcastic reference to Chinese President Hu Jintao's calls for a "harmonious society." Soon, the censors caught on and added "harmonized" to the blacklist.

The Chinese term for "harmonized" is *he xie*—which sounds the same as the Chinese term for "river crabs" but with a slightly different intonation. Now, Chinese online chatter frequently includes references to river crabs—the latest code for censorship, says MacKinnon, who studies the Chinese Internet at the University of Hong Kong.

Xia says he's confident the "hacktivists" can win their cat-and-mouse game with the Chinese authorities. After all, he says, the Chinese zodiac favors rodents in 2008: "It's the Year of the Rat."

> *"If China blocks access, it will finally make clear to the Chinese people who is pulling the levers of censorship in the country."*

Google Ends Internet Censorship, Dares China to Make Next Move

Michael B. Farrell

Michael B. Farrell is a staff writer for the Christian Science Monitor. *In this viewpoint, Farrell reports that after operating in China since 2006, Google, the giant US-based search engine company, moved its servers to Hong Kong. According to Farrell, Google had been complying with China's Internet policies, which required Google to censor search results. The move to nearby Hong Kong, the author says, will allow Chinese citizens to use Google uncensored.*

As you read, consider the following questions:

1. To where did Google move its China search operations, as reported in the viewpoint?

2. When did Google first reluctantly enter China, according to Farrell?

3. What do Google officials and watchers say that China is doing as Internet use grows?

After two months of negotiations with Chinese officials over the country's Internet censorship rules, Google pulled the plug on its China-based website Monday and began redirecting traffic to an uncensored site based in Hong Kong.

Google said it would quit adhering to Chinese web filtering policies after discovering it was targeted in a sophisticated cyber attack originating from China and that Gmail accounts belonging to Chinese human rights activists were routinely compromised.

While the Mountain View, Calif., search giant said in a statement that it hopes to keep sales and research and development operations in China, the move to circumvent the censors certainly puts its presence there on rocky footing.

The decision to host its search operation in Hong Kong could be a precursor to a complete departure from China, potentially cutting Google off from the country's 400 million users—the world's biggest Web audience.

"We want as many people in the world as possible to have access to our services, including users in mainland China, yet the Chinese government has been crystal clear throughout our discussions that self-censorship is a non-negotiable legal requirement," said David Drummond, Google's chief legal officer, in the statement.

"We believe this new approach of providing uncensored search in simplified Chinese from Google.com.hk is a sensible solution to the challenges we've faced—it's entirely legal and will meaningfully increase access to information for people in China," he said.

The Chinese government has yet to respond to Google's decision, which is being hailed by many online free speech advocates.

"Whether the Chinese people will be able to take advantage of Google search now rests squarely with the Chinese government," said Leslie Harris, president and CEO of the Center for Democracy and Technology, in a statement. "If China blocks access, it will finally make clear to the Chinese people who is pulling the levers of censorship in the country."

Others suggest that Google could be the first wave of technology companies taking a firmer stance against censorship.

According to the *Washington Post*, Sen. Richard Durbin (D-Ill.) is considering a bill that would require "Internet companies to take reasonable steps to protect human rights, or face civil and criminal liability."

Google entered China in 2006 somewhat reluctantly. While the company was uneasy with Chinese censorship rules, it accepted the policies, hoping the value of its other services would benefit the Chinese people and that censorship laws would eventually ease.

But according to Google officials and China watchers, the country's grip on online information has been tightening as Internet usage continues to climb.

Moving Google's Chinese search site to Hong Kong raises many legal questions, according to Danny Sullivan, editor of Search Engine Land. Even though Hong Kong enjoys a large degree of independence from Beijing, the Chinese government could potentially take steps to block Google servers.

"It all comes down to whether the Chinese government decides operating off a Hong Kong domain—rather than the main Chinese domain—lets Google get around its censorship rules," Mr. Sullivan wrote Monday.

Periodical and Internet Sources Bibliography

The following articles have been selected to supplement the diverse views presented in this chapter.

James Ball	"Hacktivists in the Frontline Battle for the Internet," *The Guardian* (Manchester, UK), April 20, 2012.
Judson Berger	"US Government Slips Through China Internet Censors with New Technology," Fox News, February 5, 2011. www.foxnews.com.
Ty McCormick	"Hacktivism: A Short History," *Foreign Policy*, May–June 2013.
Robert McMahon and Isabella Bennett	"US Internet Providers and the 'Great Firewall' of China," Council on Foreign Relations, February 23, 2011. www.cfr.org.
Michael Moran	"From Short Waves to Flash Mobs," *Slate*, April 10, 2012. www.slate.com.
New York Times	"Enabling China," July 24, 2011.
Cinnamon Nippard	"International Hacktivists Help Syrian Citizens Circumvent Internet Censorship," Deutsche Welle, August 18, 2011. www.dw.de.
Nick Schulz	"For a New Approach to China," Mint, January 17, 2010. www.livemint.com.
Tom Scott	"Web Filtering: Why a Great British Firewall Will Be Useless," *The Guardian* (Manchester, UK), December 20, 2010.
Somini Sengupta	"The Soul of the New Hacktivist," *New York Times*, March 17, 2012.
John Tozzi	"A Startup's Tool Helps Evade Iran's Censors, for Now," *Bloomberg BusinessWeek*, April 11, 2012. www.businessweek.com.

OPPOSING
VIEWPOINTS®
SERIES

CHAPTER 4

Which Legal Measures Effectively Address Internet Censorship?

Chapter Preface

On May 12, 2011, US senator Patrick Leahy introduced PIPA (Preventing Real Online Threats to Economic Creativity and Theft of Intellectual Property Act; also known as PROTECT IP Act) to the United States Senate. PIPA was a bill that would provide the US government and copyright holders the power to curb public access to "rogue websites dedicated to infringing or counterfeiting goods." A similar House version of the bill, known as SOPA (Stop Online Piracy Act), was introduced in the House of Representatives on October 26, 2011. Both PIPA and SOPA proved to be controversial proposals, sparking passionate debates about Internet censorship and the protection of online speech.

Copyright infringement and the sale of counterfeit goods on the Internet are widely acknowledged to be serious problems that need to be addressed. Senator Leahy underscored the extent of the problem in a January 2011 statement. "Rogue websites, primarily based overseas, are stealing American property, harming American consumers, hurting the American economic recovery and costing us American jobs," he stated. "Stealing and counterfeiting are wrong. They are harmful. The Institute for Policy Innovation estimates that copyright infringement alone costs more than $50 billion a year, and the sale of counterfeits online is estimated to be several times more costly. The AFL-CIO [labor union coalition] estimates that hundreds of thousands of jobs are lost to these forms of theft."

The introduction of PIPA and SOPA led to immediate opposition from a number of free-speech activists, civil-liberties groups, online entrepreneurs, and technology companies. This coalition expressed concern that the bills' definition of "rogue websites" was too vague and that tech companies would be forced to police the Internet. Opponents of the bills organized an "Internet blackout" on January 18, 2012, in which an estimated 75,000 websites—including the popular sites Wikipedia, Google, Reddit, BoingBoing, and Wired—protested both PIPA and SOPA by going dark or posting a message to users to contact their congressional representatives to voice their opposition to the bills. According to the White House, 103,785 people signed petitions to kill the bills that day.

The blackout protests had an immediate effect. By January 20, a number of senators had withdrawn their support for PIPA and announced their opposition. In the House of Representatives, there was a similar effect regarding SOPA. Senate majority leader Harry Reid announced that a vote on PIPA would be postponed indefinitely. SOPA was also pulled from a vote by House Judiciary Committee chairman Lamar Smith.

In May 2011, Senator Ron Wyden put a hold on PIPA in the Senate, which prevented the legislation from advancing to a Senate vote. In a public statement he outlined his opposition to the bill. "The Internet represents the shipping land of the 21st century. It is increasingly in America's economic interest to ensure that the Internet is a viable means for American innovation, commerce, and the advancement for our ideals that empower people all around the world. By ceding control of the Internet to corporations through a private right of action, and to government agencies that do not sufficiently understand and value the Internet, PIPA represents a threat to our economic future and to our international objectives."

Although SOPA and PIPA were shelved indefinitely, US legislators have not given up on crafting antipiracy legislation that would protect American consumers and businesses from rogue websites. The success of the coalition opposed to SOPA and PIPA, however, seems to show that these legislators must be very careful in developing a law that protects Internet freedom.

The debate over antipiracy bills like SOPA and PIPA is one of the subjects debated in the following chapter on the controversy over legal measures related to Internet censorship.

> *"The newly-amended Global Online Freedom Act (GOFA), . . . while far from perfect, is an important step toward protecting human rights and free expression online."*

The Global Online Freedom Act 2012 Is an Important Step Forward

Cindy Cohn, Jillian C. York, and Trevor Timm

Cindy Cohn is general counsel and legal director for the Electronic Frontier Foundation (EFF), Jillian C. York is director for international freedom of expression for the EFF, and Trevor Timm is an activist with the EFF. In the following viewpoint, the authors assert that the newly amended Global Online Freedom Act 2012 (GOFA) is a crucial step toward protecting human rights and free expression online. The authors enumerate concerns that the EFF has with the bill, including the bill's lack of transparency and a vulnerability to politicization. The EFF also objects to the inclusion of intellectual property issues in the bill, which they contend make GOFA look like silly political pan-

dering. Overall, however, they conclude that it is a significant improvement over earlier versions of the bill, and with some clarification and other tweaking the EFF may come to support it.

As you read, consider the following questions:

1. According to the authors, Internet technology companies were prohibited from selling web-filtering software to what countries as dictated in the 2007 version of the Global Online Freedom Act (GOFA)?

2. What does Section 103 of GOFA dictate, according to Cohn, York, and Timm?

3. What concerns do the authors say the EFF has with the Safe Harbor provision of the bill?

Over the past decade, and particularly in the past year, media and civil society have had success through naming and shaming companies acting as "repression's little helper": U.S. and E.U. [European Union] companies who have helped authoritarian countries censor the Internet and surveil their citizens with sophisticated technology. Today, EFF [Electronic Frontier Foundation] published a whitepaper outlining our suggestions for how companies selling surveillance and filtering technologies can avoid assisting repressive regimes.

In that vein, the newly-amended Global Online Freedom Act (GOFA), just passed by a House Sub-Committee, while far from perfect, is an important step toward protecting human rights and free expression online.

This is not the first time that GOFA has been proposed, nor is it even the first time the bill has been approved by the House Sub-Committee; a 2007 version, which literally named the countries to which filtering technology would be restricted (Belarus, Cuba, Ethiopia, Iran, Laos, North Korea, the People's Republic of China, Tunisia, and Vietnam), was also approved by the House but never came to the floor for a vote.

In the past, EFF has had extreme reservations about GOFA, in part because it sought to add more items to the U.S. export restrictions, which could easily mean that activists and people seeking to secure their own networks would lose out more than repressive governments. But in many respects, GOFA has come a long way, thanks in large part to the efforts of its authors in seeking feedback from the tech community and civil society. The bill still needs more definitions and clearer definitions of key terms, and we are not yet ready to support it, but we'll be watching it closely. The current version of GOFA would:

1. Require government assessments of "freedom of expression with respect to electronic information in each foreign country."

2. Require disclosure from companies about their human rights practices, to be evaluated by an independent third party.

3. Limit the export of technologies that "serve the primary purpose of" facilitating government surveillance or censorship to governments in countries designated as "Internet-restricting."

Transparency

But let's take a deeper look . . .

The bill contains a number of excellent measures that would ultimately encourage more transparency amongst software and hardware companies, as well as online service providers. The companies involved have been notoriously secretive and have often refused comment to reporters when their products have been found in authoritarian regimes.

Section 103 of the bill would require that the human rights reports already written for each country by the State Department include assessments of country's Internet freedom, including the availability of Internet access, and government attempts to filter or censor nonviolent, political, or religious expression. Section 103 would also require assessments about the extent to which authorities in a given country have sought information on an individual or group relevant to their nonviolent activities, as well as the electronic surveillance practices of a given country.

These assessments—undertaken by U.S. diplomatic personnel—would also include the input of human rights organizations, technology and Internet companies, and other "appropriate nongovernmental organizations [NGOs]." The inclusion of NGOs is an important addition, since we are concerned that the State Department process could be vulnerable to politicization. Because of this, we'd like to see the role of nongovernmental organizations increase as the bill develops further. Additionally, since the most robust research on Internet censorship and surveillance has come from the academic community and independent researchers, these must be added too.

Importantly, the bill should also be extended to require transparency from all companies providing tools and services that can be used for surveillance and censorship, and not just companies providing Internet communications services. Transparency from technology vendors and providers of other services is as important as transparency from Internet service providers. In fact, the transparency sections also can and should reach a broader range of technologies and companies than the export restrictions, which should remain narrow if they are to exist at all. As a result, we recommend decoupling the transparency and export restrictions.

Human Rights Standards for Companies

We also commend Sec. 201, which sets up a good framework for human rights due diligence procedures for companies operating "in any Internet-restricting country" (a designation upon which we will comment below). It requires reports that

The History of the Global Online Freedom Act

First introduced in 2006 as H.R. 4780, the Global Online Freedom Act (GOFA) has evolved through four congresses and reportedly has faced resistance from both the Administration and industry. Since its introduction, various versions of the bill have sought the following: to establish an Office of Global Internet Freedom (OGIF); to require the Administration to submit an annual report on "Internet-restricting countries" and U.S. efforts to counter such interference; and to prevent U.S. companies from cooperating with governments that engage in censorship and other human rights abuses. Key provisions have included prohibiting U.S. companies from the following: storing personally identifiable information in Internet-restricting countries; providing such information to officials of such countries; and jamming U.S.-supported websites or content, subject to civil and criminal penalties (or to waivers in some cases). Under some versions of the bill, a U.S. business that provided a search engine or content hosting service in an Internet-restricting country would be required to disclose to the OGIF all information or data related to the censorship of information in response to the policies of that country.

Thomas Lumm, Patricia Moloney Figliola,
and Matthew C. Weed, Congressional Research Service,
July 13, 2012.

must be approved by the most senior level of a company, and independently assessed by a third party. These reports would be made either to the Securities [and] Exchange Commission [SEC] or to a multi-stakeholder initiative that conducts independent third-party audits. Unfortunately, only the SEC reports are to be made publicly available online (with an exception for classified information). This should be fixed, but otherwise, the human rights due diligence standards are similar to those in the Human Rights and Technology Sales standards EFF has published today.

All of the aforementioned reports are to be constructed on the basis of Article 19 of the International Covenant on Civil and Political Rights, which states that everyone should have the right to: hold opinions without interference, freedom of expression (including the freedom to seek, receive, and impart information and ideas of all kinds, regardless of frontiers and through the media of his/her choice).

Internet-Restricting Countries

While there is much to like in GOFA, we still have extreme reservations about giving the Secretary of State sole authority to determine that a country is an "internet-restricting country." The Secretary is to determine, based on the review of evidence, whether the government of the country is "directly or indirectly" responsible for a systematic pattern of substantial restrictions on Internet freedom during any part of the preceding 1-year period. As we noted above, one way to help mediate that is to increase the role of non-governmental organizations, academic institutions and independent researchers.

More transparency should also be injected into this process. Already a description of evidence used by the Secretary of State to make the determination, as well as all unclassified portions of the report must be posted online, which is good. Unfortunately, this only applies to countries placed on the "internet-restricting countries" list. The Secretary of State should include information about countries left *off* the list: Politics and diplomatic pressure can cut both ways. To better ward off claims of politicization, the public should be able to see the evidence for why a country has *or* has not been included.

We also have concerns about the "Safe Harbor" provision of the bill, in Sec. 201(a)(3), which would allow companies to circumvent reporting requirements by joining the Global Network Initiative (GNI) or another multi-stakeholder group (defined in the bill as a group made up of civil society, human rights organizations, and companies, and committed to promoting the rule of law, free expression, and privacy). While as members of the GNI, we believe that membership in it or similar initiatives should be encouraged, companies should not be given a pass for reporting to the public or fulfilling any other requirements merely for joining such groups. The Safe Harbor could still allow the companies to avoid reporting to the SEC, but it must not allow them to avoid public reporting. Moreover, companies should have to participate in a Multi-Stakeholder group as defined in the bill under section 201(a)(3)(B), including having an independent body provide honest analysis of a company's exports laid out in the bill. The GNI could be one such group, of course, but it shouldn't have special status.

Export Restrictions

We also continue to be concerned about the export restrictions, although the bill is now much less worrisome than it once was. The authors, smartly, now propose only a very limited export restriction that reaches only sales to government end users in Internet restricting countries. As an organization with a long history of fighting the overbroad application of export restrictions, we're still concerned, but the limited scope here can at least minimize the chances that these regulations could hinder activists in foreign countries from getting, for instance, technologies that can help them monitor their own communications for security vulnerabilities and backdoors. We will need to watch this process carefully, though. At a minimum, the bill should create a very clear and simple process for those seeking to provide technologies to people overseas to challenge any agency action that oversteps this narrow category.

A Broad Waiver Provision

We're also concerned about the broad waiver provision. It allows the President on a case-by-case basis to certify to Congress that "it is in the national interests of the United States to" issue an exemption. We think the President should have to justify any waiver publicly, to the extent that any part of the analysis is not classified. Also, the standard should be more robust than just the recitation of "national interests." That is too easily abused.

It's not hard to see that much of the technology that was misused by governments during the "Arab Spring" was originally sold to countries that were "allies" of the U.S. at the time. Yet, most of these technologies were easily and quickly used to suppress dissent of citizens. A prime example is Egypt, which likely was an ally of the U.S. when it purchased the Narus surveillance technologies used against democracy activists. Similarly, Libya bought technology from France under the guise of fighting terrorism, but used the technology to surveil activists, human rights campaigners, and journalists. Would such a waiver provision be used for Bahrain—still a staunch ally of the U.S.—where several cases have emerged in which activists were tortured while being read transcripts of their text messages and phone calls?

Why Include Intellectual Property?

Finally, for no good reason the bill now references intellectual property: "No provision under this Act shall be construed to affect a country's ability to adopt measures designed to combat infringement of intellectual property." This provision appears to have no substantive impact, but instead appears to have been included to appease Congressional offices (and their content industry patrons) that seemingly require that intellectual property be mentioned in any law that also mentions the Internet. Frankly, the inclusion of this provision makes Congress look unserious. It simply has no place in a legislative proposal aimed at curbing the use of technology to aid in torture, summary execution and other deadly serious human rights abuses. It should be removed.

| "GOFA needs refining."

Internet Freedom Starts at Home

Rebecca MacKinnon

Rebecca MacKinnon is a journalist, a Schwartz senior fellow at the liberal think tank the New America Foundation, cofounder of the citizen media network Global Voices, and author of a book on global Internet freedom. In the following viewpoint, she suggests that a recent bill that forbids US Internet technology companies to sell web-filtering and surveillance technology to "Internet-restricting countries" is fundamentally flawed. MacKinnon points out that although the Global Online Freedom Act (GOFA) 2012 targets authoritarian and repressive governments, it fails to address the growing problem of democratically elected governments that are abusing their censorship and surveillance powers. Countries like India, Great Britain, and the United States have been increasingly proactive in Internet censorship and surveillance with the collaboration of US Internet technology companies, MacKinnon contends. By forging such an opaque and unaccountable relationship, she says, the US government and American industry are forging a path toward more Internet censorship around the world.

Rebecca MacKinnon, "Internet Freedom Starts at Home," *Foreign Policy*, April 3, 2012.

As you read, consider the following questions:

1. According to MacKinnon, what country is the biggest customer of American-made surveillance technology?

2. What concerns does the Center for Democracy and Technology have with the Global Online Freedom Act, according to the author?

3. According to an investigation by the American Civil Liberties Union, cited by MacKinnon, what are US police departments across the nation doing that violates the law?

"An electronic curtain has fallen around Iran," U.S. President Barack Obama warned in a video message marking the Persian New Year. Government censorship and surveillance, he said, make it more difficult for Iranians to "access the information that they want," denying "the rest of the world the benefit of interacting with the Iranian people."

Implied though not explicit in Obama's remarks was the idea that if Iran's Internet were freer and more open, Iran's relationship with the world generally—and the United States in particular—would be different. Cases like Iran are the main driver of Washington's bipartisan consensus around the idea that a free and open global Internet is in the United States' strategic interest.

Yet more than two years after Secretary of State Hillary Clinton gave her first speech declaring "Internet freedom" to be a major component of U.S. foreign policy, it turns out that many of the most sophisticated tools used to suppress online free speech and dissent around the world are actually Made in the USA. American corporations are major suppliers of software and hardware used by all sorts of governments to carry out censorship and surveillance—and not just dictatorships. Inconveniently, governments around the democratic world are pushing to expand their own censorship and surveillance powers as they struggle to address genuine problems related to cybercrime, cyberwar, child protection, and intellectual property.

Even more inconveniently, the U.S. government is the biggest and most powerful customer of American-made surveillance technology, shaping the development of those technologies as well as the business practices and norms for public-private collaboration around them. As long as the U.S. government continues to support the development of a surveillance-technology industry that clearly lacks concern for the human rights and civil liberties implications of its business—even rewarding secretive and publicly unaccountable behavior by these companies—the world's dictators will remain well supplied by a robust global industry.

American-made technology has turned up around the Middle East and North Africa over the past year—from Syria to Bahrain to Saudi Arabia, from pre-revolutionary Tunisia to Egypt—in contexts that leave no doubt that the software and hardware in question were being used to censor dissenting speech and track activists. While much of this technology is considered "dual use" because it can be used to defend computer networks against cyberattack as well as to censor and monitor political speech, some members of Congress are seeking to prevent its use for political repression. To that end, the Global Online Freedom Act (GOFA), which passed through the House of Representatives Subcommittee on Africa, Global Health, and Human Rights last week, takes aim not only at U.S.-headquartered companies but also overseas companies funded by U.S. capital markets.

As GOFA's sponsor, Rep. Chris Smith of New Jersey, bluntly put it, repressive regimes in Iran, China, and Syria "are transforming the Internet into a 'weapon of mass surveillance.'" The bill has been kicking around Congress in various forms since 2006 after Yahoo handed over dissidents' email account information to the Chinese authorities and other companies, including Cisco, Microsoft, and Google, came under fire for aiding Chinese political censorship to varying degrees. While its specifics have changed over the years, the current version contains three main elements:

1. It requires the State Department to create a list of "Internet-restricting countries."

2. It requires that all companies listed on U.S. stock exchanges disclose to the Securities and Exchange Commission what procedures and practices they have put in place to protect the free expression and privacy rights of users in "Internet-restricting" countries.

3. It revises U.S. export control laws to forbid the export of censorship and surveillance technology to "Internet-restricting countries."

GOFA has received ringing endorsements from a number of human rights groups as well as from Yahoo—which, after a few years of humiliation in Congress and the media over its mistakes in China, has made a public commitment to human rights. The second part of the bill, focused on corporate transparency, is modeled after sections 1502 and 1504 of the recently passed Dodd-Frank Act, which requires conflict-minerals and extractive-revenue disclosure. It is based on the premise that at least some investors care about the human rights responsibilities of U.S.-listed businesses. More broadly, the idea is that just as companies are expected to commit to basic environmental, labor, and human rights standards when it comes to their operations in the physical world, investors, consumers, and government regulators should expect similar commitments to users' and customers' rights to digital free expression and privacy when using the Internet and mobile devices.

Companies that join the Global Network Initiative (GNI), a multi-stakeholder organization through which Internet and telecommunications companies work with human rights groups, socially responsible investors, and academics to uphold core principles on free expression, privacy, and human rights, would receive "safe harbor" from this requirement. So far only five companies have joined the GNI: Google, Microsoft, Yahoo, Websense, and Evoca. (Full disclosure: I am on the GNI's board of directors.) It is possible that the bill will be an incentive for more companies to join the GNI even if it fails to pass.

Some free speech groups, however, have stopped short of a full-on endorsement of the bill. The Center for Democracy and Technology, while supportive of its general aims, cautions that GOFA needs refining in order to prevent unintended restrictions on the sale of badly needed technology to activists and NGOs working in authoritarian countries. Existing laws already fail to get the balance right: The Electronic Frontier Foundation is campaigning to reform current trade sanctions that are preventing opposition activists in countries like Syria from accessing U.S. companies' software and communications tools. The digital freedom group Access shares these concerns and also worries that the State Department's list of "Internet-restricting countries" will become politicized, potentially absolving companies that assist U.S. allies in censoring and monitoring political dissent.

The bill's drafters have further created problems for themselves by combining export controls and transparency requirements in one piece of legislation that applies to the same list of "Internet-restricting" countries. Export controls by nature target a list of countries that, due to U.S. trade and diplomatic interests and political lobbying by companies, is inevitably a relatively short list focused on the worst offenders. Thus the export control section of the bill will create pressure on the State Department to keep the list of "Internet-restricting" countries as short as possible.

Yet the bill's transparency requirements will lose much of their force and meaning unless they target corporate-government collaboration in a much wider range of countries where governments attempt to abuse censorship and surveillance powers. Consider, for example, India, the world's largest democracy—which is unlikely to be placed on a State Department "Internet-restricting countries" list making it subject to sanctions—but where the government is making increasingly aggressive demands of Internet companies to censor content and hand over user information. Or Britain, where civil liberties groups are in an uproar over plans by Prime Minister David Cameron's government to introduce a law enabling the government to monitor calls, emails, texts, and website visits of everyone in the country without a court order or warrant. Under GOFA, companies are unlikely to be held responsible for assisting these democratically elected governments in abusing their censorship and surveillance powers.

In congressional testimony last December, I argued that the section of GOFA requiring companies to adopt and disclose measures to protect Internet users' free expression and privacy rights should be based on a universal standard, not just the State Department's whim. The Global Network Initiative, for example, applies a global standard to corporate-government interactions. Why? Because the initiative's members—who include a range of civil liberties groups, human rights organizations, socially responsible investors, and academics—cannot come up with a single country where the abuse of free expression and privacy by government and corporations is not a genuine concern.

All companies doing business everywhere—including in the United States—should commit to uphold and defend the free expression and privacy rights of their users for the same reasons we expect other types of companies agree to respect the health and safety of the people who purchase and consume their products. Companies should be required to demonstrate that commitment by reporting publicly not only on how they gather and retain user information, but also how and under what circumstances they share that information

The Battle for Internet Freedom

Control of the Internet also includes the ability to exert censorship restrictions. Some of the world's governments seek to censor, intercept, decode, disrupt, guard, or otherwise control Internet traffic. In several countries, Internet control implies the monitoring and control of the Internet behaviors of its citizens. For example, the government of China employs more than 30,000 full-time workers to monitor Internet systems accessed by the country's 250 million Web users. In the past, China has periodically blocked access to various websites, including Wikipedia, United Nations News, and the human-rights group Amnesty International. The OpenNet Initiative asserts that close to forty-five countries filter or heavily censor the Internet for political content or individual speech. Most countries have restrictive Internet laws that limit the content available to children in school or ban the illegal transfer of copyrighted materials.

Global Issues in Context,
"Internet Control and Security," 2013.
www.gale.cengage.com.

with governments as well as other companies. Only then can people have a clear sense of how power is being exercised over their digital lives and know whom to hold accountable when that power is abused.

But GOFA, by targeting corporate sales and government relationships in the worst-case countries while skirting the much more inconvenient question of how companies facilitate government abuse of surveillance and censorship powers in democracies and close U.S. allies, completely sidesteps the root of the problem: the main market drivers whose demand for surveillance technology is actually shaping and funding the development of these technologies.

Make no mistake: American tech companies are up to their eyeballs in bad behavior. Despite industry and government efforts to keep the media in the dark about a traveling trade show for surveillance technology known as the "Wiretappers' Ball," recent media reports have revealed the extent to which American corporate innovations in surveillance technology are driven by U.S. government demand. And the U.S. government is by far those companies' biggest customer.

According to the *Washington Post*, at last year's trade show just outside Washington in Northern Virginia, 35 federal agencies as well as representatives from state and local law enforcement mixed with representatives of 43 countries. Despite the Obama administration's proclaimed commitment to Internet freedom, the executive branch of the U.S. government makes no effort to be honest or transparent with the American public about the types of surveillance technologies it is sourcing and purchasing, what capabilities these technologies have, or which other governments are purchasing these technologies.

What this means for American democracy—let alone for the democratic aspirations of people anywhere else—became abundantly clear this past Sunday, April 1, when the *New York Times* reported on a detailed investigation by the American Civil Liberties Union that uncovered widespread use of cell-phone tracking technology by police departments around the country in non-emergency situations without court orders or warrants.

Meanwhile, as GOFA moves forward, Congress is considering several cybersecurity bills that would authorize Internet service providers and other companies not only to monitor private communications passing over their networks, but also to share private communications with the National Security Agency and other federal entities or with any other agency of the federal government designated by the Department of

Homeland Security—and with less due process and judicial oversight than ever before. While acknowledging that cybersecurity is a legitimate goal, groups focused on the defense and protection of Internet users' rights, including the Center for Democracy and Technology and the Electronic Frontier Foundation, have expressed deep-seated concerns about the extent to which these bills open the door even wider for civil liberties violations.

GOFA's supporters argue that one has to start somewhere and that focusing on the relationship between U.S. companies and authoritarian dictatorships is the best way to obtain bipartisan consensus to pass legislation. That is no doubt true. But if the American people continue to allow the U.S. government and American industry to forge increasingly unaccountable and opaque relationships around the exchange and use of citizens' private information, the damage will extend well beyond American democracy and civil liberties. The business norms and technological innovations born of such opaque and unaccountable relationships will keep dictators supplied with handy tools for decades to come.

"The Stop Online Piracy Act ... does not threaten the Internet as a tool of communication and commerce [but only] the profits generated by those who willfully steal intellectual property."

The Stop Online Piracy Act Safeguards Property Rights and Does Not Threaten Internet Freedom

Lamar Smith

Lamar Smith is a Republican congressman from Texas and the sponsor of the Stop Online Piracy Act (SOPA). In the following viewpoint, he maintains that SOPA effectively addresses the problem of online criminals who steal US intellectual property and sell counterfeit products on rogue websites. Such online piracy occurs at great cost to the American economy, Smith asserts, and often results in inferior and dangerous products being sold around the world. Smith argues that SOPA has been revised to strengthen protections of Internet freedoms, and in its latest version, only the worst foreign rogue websites are targeted, and the US Justice Department must prove its cases against these sites in a court of law. Enforcing the law—whether it be online or in the real world—is not censorship, according to Smith. He concludes that much of the opposition to SOPA is self-serving because it is funded by companies that profit from doing business with rogue sites.

As you read, consider the following questions:

1. According to Smith, how many cosponsors of the Stop Online Piracy Act are there?

2. How much money does the US economy lose annually because of the theft of US intellectual property, according to estimates cited by Smith?

3. How much does the author report that Google paid to settle a criminal case because of its promotion of rogue foreign pharmacies on its search engine?

If you've read recent articles in *The Hill* regarding legislation to help stop online piracy, you might think that the sky is falling. Several of the articles extensively quote opponents of the bipartisan Stop Online Piracy Act [SOPA] without any reference to the bill's 29 bipartisan co-sponsors and numerous industry supporters.

Unfortunately, this biased reporting discredits *The Hill* as a legitimate news source and does a disservice to the readers who rely on *The Hill*'s reporting for the facts.

SOPA's Targets

So let's set the record straight.

The Stop Online Piracy Act specifically targets foreign websites primarily dedicated to illegal activity or foreign websites that market themselves as such. The bill addresses the problem of online criminals who steal and sell America's intellectual property [IP] and keep the profits for themselves.

When most Americans think about counterfeit goods, they think about street vendors who sell fake brand-name purses or pirated DVDs for a fraction of the price. But what many Americans don't realize is that there is a vast virtual market online run by criminals who steal products and profits that rightly belong to American innovators.

These foreign websites are called "rogue sites" because they are out of reach of U.S. laws. Movies and music are not the only stolen products that are offered by rogue sites. Counterfeit medicine, automotive parts and even baby food are a big part of the counterfeiting business, and pose a serious threat to the health of American consumers.

Because the U.S. produces the most intellectual property, our nation has the most to lose if we fail to address the problem of rogue sites. According to estimates, IP theft costs the U.S. economy more than $100 billion annually and results in the loss of thousands of American jobs.

Key Revisions to SOPA

The recently introduced manager's amendment to the Stop Online Piracy Act makes clear that the legislation specifically targets the worst-of-the-worst foreign rogue websites. Legitimate and lawful websites like Facebook, YouTube and Twitter have nothing to worry about under this bill.

In fact, the changes in the manager's amendment reflect conversations with representatives from companies like Microsoft and Facebook, and seek to address technical concerns with the first draft. The resulting manager's amendment improves the legislation, increases industry support and ensures the protection of American innovation and American jobs.

Under the bill, only the Justice Department can seek an injunction against a foreign website for which the primary purpose is illegal and infringing activity. The Justice Department must go to court and lay out the case against the site. If the judge finds that the site is primarily engaged in illegal activity, a court order can be issued that authorizes the Justice Department to request that the site be blocked. Internet Ser-

PIPA and SOPA

In May 2011, the U.S. Senate Judiciary Committee approved a bill titled "Preventing Real Online Threats to Economic Creativity and Theft of Intellectual Property Act" (also known as the Protect IP Act, or PIPA), which allows copyright holders to suppress or disrupt search engine links to sites with a pattern and practice of copyright infringement. The Bill awaits approval by the full Senate and reconciliation with similar House bills before becoming law. The Bill seeks to limit traffic referrals and disrupt payments to sites allegedly engaging in digital piracy or selling counterfeit goods. Critics contended that the bill is flawed because the threshold for action remains unclear and that only large media companies would be able to fight indiscriminate or false claims by alleged copyright holders.

On 18 January 2012, numerous websites launched protests against the Stop Online Piracy Act (SOPA), PIPA's companion bill in the U.S. House of Representatives. Websites participating in the protest encouraged visitors to contact their elected representatives. Other websites, including the English-language version of Wikipedia, blacked out their websites for twenty-four hours. In the wake of the protests, five U.S. senators withdrew their support of PIPA, and U.S. Senate majority leader Harry Reid announced a postponement of the vote on PIPA.

Global Issues in Context,
"Internet Control and Security," 2013.
www.gale.cengage.com.

vice Providers and search engines will simply be required to remove the link to an illegal site so that it doesn't come up as part of the search results.

Defining Censorship

Some critics have claimed that this "blocking" of an illegal foreign site amounts to censorship of the Internet. But simply because the illegal activity occurs online does not mean that it is protected speech. Laws are enforced in the brick and mortar world. It's not censorship to enforce the law online.

The rest of the bill focuses on stopping the flow of revenue to rogue sites. If a federal judge agrees that a foreign site is dedicated to illegal and infringing activity, then a court order can be issued directing companies to sever ties with the illegal website. Third-party intermediaries, like credit card companies and online ad providers, are only required to stop working with the site. They cannot be held liable for the illegal or infringing actions taken by the rogue website.

Opposition Is Self-Serving

Unfortunately, some critics of this legislation have made large profits by promoting rogue websites that sell counterfeit goods directly to U.S. consumers. Google recently paid half a billion dollars to settle a criminal case because of the search engine giant's active promotion of rogue foreign pharmacies that sold counterfeit and illegal drugs to U.S. patients. Their opposition to this legislation is self-serving because they profit from doing business with rogue sites that steal and sell America's intellectual property.

Despite a few vocal opponents, the Stop Online Piracy Act has broad bipartisan support in Congress and across the country.

This bill does not threaten the Internet as a tool of communication and commerce. But it does threaten the profits generated by those who willfully steal intellectual property by trafficking in counterfeit or pirated goods.

> "Not only would [SOPA] likely do little to address the problem of online content fraud and counterfeiting, but it takes aim at the core features of the Internet."

The Stop Online Piracy Act Threatens Internet Freedom and Does Not Protect Property Rights

Nancy Scola

Nancy Scola is a journalist and correspondent for The Atlantic. *In the following viewpoint, she reports that the US Internet community is united in its opposition to the Stop Online Piracy Act (SOPA) because it threatens Internet freedom. Scola contends that the bill, designed to address the problem of online content fraud and counterfeiting, is fundamentally flawed because it targets search engines, Internet service providers, ad and payment networks—all of which are crucial to Internet functioning. In addition, Scola says, SOPA is ineffective in protecting intellectual property and counterfeiting from a technical perspective. Con-*

gress should not pass a bill that will not effectively address the problem but would instead threaten the very infrastructure of the Internet just to placate the US entertainment industry, she concludes.

As you read, consider the following questions:

1. According to Scola, what leading US Internet companies oppose the Stop Online Piracy Act?
2. What do safe harbor provisions do, according to the author?
3. How much money does Scola report that the entertainment companies and other SOPA allies spent in 2010 and 2011 on lobbying activities?

Ever since the days of Napster [an early peer-to-peer music sharing service], the recording industry and movie industry have treated the Internet as a place on the map marked "Here be dragons." For the last decade, Hollywood and big music have spent time not innovating, but trying to get the U.S. Congress to help them tame the Internet. Over the years, they've floated a variety of legislative mechanisms to do that. The latest is a House bill called the Stop Online Piracy Act. SOPA, as it is known, has Internet advocates boiling—and with good reason.

A Controversial Bill

While the Motion Picture Association of America and its allies rolled out their attorney, First Amendment lawyer Floyd Abrams, to say that the bill would "protect creators of speech, as Congress has done since this nation was founded, by combating its theft," many in the technology world roared disapproval. At Techdirt, Mike Masnick compared SOPA to the Internet restrictions used by repressive regimes; "Setting up such a system in the US would be an epic mistake," he wrote.

GigaOm's Mathew Ingram wrote that the bill gives the government and private companies "unprecedented powers to remove websites on the flimsiest of grounds." The Electronic Frontier Foundation called the bill "a dangerous wish list." The nonprofit Center for Democracy and Technology in Washington said SOPA would cause "broad collateral damage to freedom of expression and privacy."

Leading Internet companies, including AOL, eBay, Facebook, Google, LinkedIn, Mozilla, Twitter, Yahoo and Zynga, teamed up in a Washington-speak letter drily objecting to the bill. Google's Eric Schmidt was blunter. "The solutions are draconian," he said in an appearance at MIT [Massachusetts Institute of Technology]. The bill "would require ISPs [Internet service providers] to remove URLs [website addresses] from the Web, which is also known as censorship last time I checked."

When it comes to talking about SOPA, it is important to remember this: You can think that "intellectual property" infringement (not only of movies and music, but knockoff Nikes sold online) is bad for the American economy and still think the legislation is a disaster. Not only would the bill likely do little to address the problem of online content fraud and counterfeiting, but it takes aim at the core features of the Internet that have contributed a great deal to the American economy.

An Epic Battle

Congress, the political press and lobbyists for the entertainment industries like to frame this fight as one between giants. In one corner, the MPAA [Motion Picture Association of America], RIAA [Recording Industry Association of America] and others decrying the "lawlessness" of the Internet and in the other, Google, Facebook and other big tech firms defending their business. But SOPA isn't just about corporate battles. For all the the rhetoric, this isn't even really about copyright.

This is about the Internet—and more to the point, the infrastructure and operations of the Internet that make the Internet the Internet. SOPA targets search engines, Internet service providers, ad networks and payment networks precisely because those components are so central to the functioning of the Internet. Those are digital forces that should be messed with only with the greatest of care.

Here, in a nutshell, is what SOPA does. Under the bill, the U.S. attorney general can, with court approval, require that search engines, ISPs, and advertising networks and payment companies stop dealing with foreign-based websites that are deeply engaged in copyright infringement, including blocking a website's name from connecting back to the site's IP [Internet protocol] address. Google, for example, could be forced to block listings for targeted sites. Other sections of the bill puts copyright holders in a position to demand that ad and payment networks stop doing business with websites based in the United States and abroad when those sites are found to have engaged in prohibited behavior when it comes to copyright.

Critics say that the bill is so broadly written that it incriminates sites that are designed in such a way that make policing copyright difficult, from Facebook to Dropbox to whatever new social network the kids in NYU's [New York University's] Interactive Telecommunications Program are cooking up. That new vulnerability might scare off not only inventors, but investors.

And, as far as the domain name parts of the bill are concerned, the approach is largely pointless from a technical perspective. The bill targets file-sharing sites like the Pirate Bay that enable users to download movies without paying. Search engines would have to excise the name. But hard-core pirates are simply going to traffic in IP addresses. For example, copy and paste "194.71.107.15" in your browser. The Pirate Bay should still pop up, and there's nothing Google can do about it. Still, the damage is done. What was once an international

system for getting around the Internet is fractured; SOPA opponents point out that it threatens to undo all the work done to harden the domain name system in federal and private cybersecurity efforts.

Safe Harbor

SOPA would overturn a long-standing presumption under U.S. law that while Internet players are certainly responsible for complying with the law, they're not deputies in the copyright battles. During a hearing in the House this week on SOPA, Maria Pallante, the U.S. register of copyrights, testified that SOPA rejects the idea that Internet companies "don't have an obligation to participate" in enforcing copyright. They don't—by design. Various U.S. laws—Section 230 of the *Communications Decency Act*, the so-called safe harbor provisions of the *Digital Millennium Copyright Act*—grant Internet companies the freedom to operate without being held responsible for knowing the legal pedigree of every piece of content on, or connected to, their sites. And for good reason.

Could Facebook have flourished with the expectation that Mark Zuckerberg and his Harvard dormmates were culpable for every link or video clip someone uploaded to their site? Not likely. So when Pallante testifies that "I believe that search engines should be fully within the reach of the attorney general," we should hear the legislation for what it is: a revision of the notion that Internet companies have a duty to comply with the law, but not to act as its enforcers.

Washington is sometimes rightfully criticized for harboring some crazy ideas when it comes to the Internet. But the federal government has gotten some basic things very right, from funding the Internet in its early stages to having the wisdom to enshrine Section 230 and the safe harbors. It would be a shame to see Congress trash that legacy with a single bill.

More Concerns About SOPA

Another concern is what SOPA would do for other countries that seek to shape the Internet as *they* see fit. China, of course, limits online discussion of democracy, often target the tools, like its homegrown version of Twitter, Sina Weibo, that foster those conversations. With SOPA, the United States would stand on shaky moral ground when it starts ordering search engines and ISPs to block and black out sites. As Secretary of State [Hillary] Clinton goes around the world promoting her "Internet Freedom Agenda," she'll be put in the position of distinguishing between the blocking of bootlegged movies (an infraction that China has shown it doesn't care much about) and limiting democratic speech online. That's a distinction very likely to get lost in translation.

And because the U.S. is doing it, there's even more at stake. We might like to think of the Internet as an organic global medium, but someone has to make the trains run on time. That someone is ICANN [Internet Corporation for Assigned Names and Numbers], a California-based group that runs the Internet's naming and numbering systems under a contract with the U.S. Department of Commerce. Not everyone in the world is pleased with the central role of the United States in the Internet's governance, with several nations and groups wanting ICANN to hand over its authority to the United Nations' International Telecommunication Union. The U.S. government—and the countless computer scientists, engineers, and Internet policy advocates who live and work here—have been good stewards of the Internet so far. SOPA would throw that away with, potentially, little in return.

Opponents of SOPA are nervous that the bill and its counterparts in the Senate have bipartisan support; SOPA's 24 co-sponsors in the House include 14 Republicans and 10 Democrats. But the sheer extremism of the measure has made for strange bedfellows. In a tweet this week, House Democratic Leader Nancy Pelosi wrote, "Need to find a better solution than #SOPA #DontBreakTheInternet." Her nemesis, Darrell Issa, Republican from California and chair of the House Oversight Committee, retweeted Pelosi's note, appending commentary of his own: "If even we can agree . . ."

So why is Congress bothering? For one thing, Congress is eager to find real solutions for the struggling American economy. And for another, the music and movie industries have spent years and millions of dollars to sell the case that online copyright infringement is an albatross around the economy that the House and Senate can make go away. Right now. Study the test of SOPA for any length of time and with any real knowledge of how the Internet works, and you'll realize it's not that simple.

The Entertainment Lobby

Still, there's a mini-industry in Washington that consists of selling the idea that it is. Using data from the Center for Responsive Politics, *Politico* recently reported that the entertainment companies and other SOPA allies spent $280 million over 2010 and 2011 on lobbying. Google, eBay, Facebook and other big tech firms, by comparison, spent $30 million. We shouldn't underestimate the degree to which SOPA is the natural product of a self-perpetuating system that demands some justification of why the MPAA *et al* are spending all those millions year after year.

Of course, at some point, even Washington has come to realize that there's a lot more to the Internet economy than that described by the movie and music industries. Google is no slouch, and no member of Congress wants to be seen as standing in the way of the next Facebook. Andrew McDiarmid, an analyst for the Center for Democracy and Technology, which opposes the bill, said, "We were kind of encouraged by the hearing this week." There were no public advocacy groups or Internet engineers testifying, and Google represented the sole opposition to the bill. "It was stacked," he said.

"But at least five members of Congress raised concerns, and they asked more questions than I think we expected," he said. "There's a fair bit of momentum on the bill, but people are really starting to take notice."

"What if we managed to create a society where at least 80% of children grow up without their sexuality being shaped by violent porn? . . . Would that be worth a try? Our answer is yes."

A Legal Ban on Violent Internet Pornography Would Benefit Children and Is Not Censorship

Halla Gunnarsdóttir

Halla Gunnarsdóttir is a journalist and political adviser to the minister of the interior in Iceland. In the following viewpoint, she commends Iceland's recent initiative to ban the online circulations of hardcore, violent pornography. After extensive consultation with academics, lawyers, law enforcement, and child protection specialists, government officials came to believe that the move was necessary to protect children from the effects of violent pornography, Gunnarsdóttir reports. Studies have shown, she says, that children exposed to such imagery can develop a distorted view of sexuality and exhibit social isolation and anxiety. Government officials aim to target only violent and degrading material and are taking concerns about Internet freedom seriously, according to Gunnarsdóttir. She contends that it is worth considering such a radical solution if it allows more children grow to up without the influence of violent Internet pornography.

As you read, consider the following questions:

1. According to the author, what is the average age that children in Iceland are first exposed to pornography?

2. What three Icelandic ministries does Gunnarsdóttir report were involved in assessing the problem of online pornography?

3. What child welfare model does Gunnarsdóttir identify as endorsed in Iceland and other Nordic countries?

The Icelandic minister of the interior's recent initiative to address the online circulation of hardcore pornography has received considerable attention from the international media. Many commentators have offered their views on the subject, some to commend the effort, others to dismiss it as well-intentioned, if misguided, or as an attempt to censor internet access in Iceland.

Assessing the Problem

The ministry's initiative emerges from an extensive consultation process on sexual violence, encompassing police, child protection specialists, lawyers and academic researchers. The experts raised concerns about the effects of porn on the nature—and possibly the scope—of sexual violence in Iceland. Research has also shown that children in Iceland are first exposed to pornography at the average age of 11. In some instances, children have been dramatically affected by it, and symptoms include social isolation and anxiety. There have also been reported cases of teenage boys re-enacting pornographic sexual acts on younger children. Finally, violent pornography is influencing teenagers' first sexual experiences.

Pornography can reach children in different ways, but it is evident that the probability of a child becoming an adult without seeing porn is close to zero. This is a matter of concern since mainstream internet porn is becoming increasingly violent and brutal. It does not simply consist of images of naked bodies, or of people having sex but of hardcore violence framed within the context of sex. Young women are usually referred to as sluts, whores, bitches etc, and represented as submissive. Men, meanwhile, often act in a dominant, degrading and violent way towards them. A fairly typical example could include a mouth-penetration, performed to produce choking, crying or even vomiting. The violent misogyny produced by the porn industry has become our children's main resource for learning what sex is about, which is a cause of serious concern.

Proposals for Policy Changes

In response to the above-mentioned expert concerns, three ministries—the ministry of the interior, the ministry of education, science and culture and the ministry of welfare—called upon a wide range of professionals to discuss and analyse the societal effects of violent pornography and to contribute to the development of a comprehensive, holistic policy. Proposals emerging from this process are now being implemented under the auspices of the three ministries. These include increased emphasis on violence prevention, revision of sex education and the forming of a comprehensive policy on sexual health. The proposals on legal amendments—now under consideration at the ministry of the interior—are, however, the ones that have received the most attention.

Firstly, a bill is being prepared with the aim of narrowing the legal definition of pornography—the distribution of which is already illegal—to encompass only violent and degrading sexual material. The goal is to make the important distinction between sex, on the one hand, and violence, on the other. This approach is based on the Norwegian penal code.

Secondly, a committee, headed by the ministry, is now exploring how the law can be implemented. The key question pertains to the possibility of placing restrictions on online distribution of violent and degrading pornography in Iceland. Under discussion are both technical solutions and legal and procedural measures.

Concerns About Censorship

Critics of this effort have argued that any such attempt automatically involves censorship and unlawful restrictions on the protected freedom of speech. It is important to emphasise that our freedom of speech and behaviour is limited in many ways, without it being considered in violation of our universal human rights. The obvious example is the general consensus on the illegality of child pornography, which includes material that does not place children directly at risk, e.g., cartoons with child-related sexual material.

Similarly, we should be able to discuss the circulation and the harmful effects of violent online pornography. And we need to be careful not to force the debate into the bipolar trenches of complete laissez-faire on the internet, on the one hand, and online censorship, on the other.

Protecting Children

Furthermore, it is argued that it should be the parents' responsibility to protect their children from unwanted material on the internet. This argument is rooted in the ongoing debate on whether society as a whole, or parents alone, should be responsible for children's welfare. International instruments support the societal approach, most notably the UN convention on the rights of the child. Such a collective approach to welfare is also one of the cornerstones of the Nordic welfare model.

All parents know that it is impossible—and far from desirable—to keep an eye on their children at all times. Internet filters for home use provide a degree of protection, but the measure is limited as children access the internet in different places and on different devices.

It has also been maintained that even the best technical solutions to limiting the distribution of violent online pornography can never be fully implemented because the porn industry will always find a way to circumvent restrictions. This might be true, as it is with respect to many issues constituting threats to public health. But what if we managed to create a society where at least 80% of children grow up without their sexuality being shaped by violent porn? What if we only manage to raise the average age of children when they are exposed to porn for the first time from 11 to 16? Would that be worth a try? Our answer is yes. That is why we are debating the topic and willing to consider radical solutions.

"Porn or not, [Iceland's] ban matters because it's censorship on a scale not yet seen on the Western web."

A Legal Ban on Internet Pornography Is Misguided and Would Lead to Internet Censorship

Derek Mead

Derek Mead is a journalist and managing editor of the website Motherboard. In the following viewpoint, he contends that a ban on Internet pornography would not work because determined users would find a way to access it. Mead also suggests that Internet porn bans, like the one that Iceland is considering, have long-reaching consequences for Internet speech. There is a problematic trend, Mead insists, of governments trying to grab control over the web by proposing ineffective legislation that reveals a troubling ignorance of how the Internet works as well as of the people who use it. Unless governments like Iceland are going to bar all access to the Internet and replace it with a state-run system, he concludes, users will be able to access anything they want.

As you read, consider the following questions:

1. According to Mead, what kind of pornography is already banned in Iceland?

2. What Middle Eastern country does the author report recently banned pornography?

3. What does Mead identify as the problem with the Cyber Intelligence Sharing and Protection Act (CISPA)?

Iceland, land of hot springs and jerk youth hockey teams, is not down with porn. The normally-left-leaning country is concerned with the effects of readily-available online porn on children and women, and thus is discussing setting up a wide-ranging set of filters—similar in concept to China's Great Firewall—to scrub the dirty web clean.

A Troubling Trend

Bummer if you're an Icelander who digs porn or a free web, but should Internet fans elsewhere be getting worked up about what a tiny Nordic country is doing? Absolutely, as it highlights a worrisome trend of Western officials' pigheaded approaches to trying to regulate the Web.

First, the dirt on Iceland's war on smut: Iceland Interior Minister Ogmundur Jonasson is currently drafting the anti-porn legislation, which reportedly (and vaguely) is designed to block access to porn by young people on any web-enabled devices. Import, publication, and distribution of offline porn is already illegal in Iceland—although the ban's murky definition of "porn" has led to hilarious vignettes of confused police—and Jonasson apparently wants to update the pre-Internet law to focus on "violent" porn. But first he wants to see if an Internet ban is even feasible.

"I want to give the committee the task of examining the legal definition of pornography," he told the *Reykjavik Grape-*

vine. "At the same time, the plan includes examining what measures the police can take to enforce the law and limit access to pornography."

Whether a complete porn ban is even possible is a question with a rather definite answer: It's not. Sure, setting up a firewall to block major porn sites is totally feasible, but also likely able to be circumvented by VPNs [virtual private networks] and the like. And even then, porn is an extremely diffuse product on the web. Would Iceland ban Reddit too? Even if it did, would it then have to ban Flickr and the stock image sites that have pictures of strippers? Facebook? It's an impossible task.

The Porn Problem

Still, Jonasson's task force is trying. Halla Gunnarsdóttir, an adviser to Jonasson, told the *Daily Mail* [of London], "at the moment, we are looking at the best technical ways to achieve this. But surely if we can send a man to the moon, we must be able to tackle porn on the Internet."

The focus of the ban appears to be on violent pornography, with Jonasson and others saying that increasingly violent pornography is harmful to those that appear in it as well as those who watch it. While "violent" isn't defined—and it's not clear if the ban would only apply to whatever violent pornography is defined as—it aligns with the thinking behind Iceland's two year old ban on strip clubs, which were considered to violate the civil rights of the women who worked in them.

"There is a strong consensus building in Iceland," Gunnarsdóttir said. "We have so many experts, from educationalists to the police and those who work with children behind this, that this has become much broader than party politics."

Gunnarsdóttir's comment is partly politicking, to be sure, but the porn ban does have its supporters. Now, that it would be the first Western nation to enact a porn ban is certainly news. And it *is* about porn, which might explain why the web has been buzzing with talk of the ban for the last week. But really, Iceland's its own country and can decide what it wants. Why should we really care?

Encroaching Censorship

Porn or not, the ban matters because it's censorship on a scale not yet seen on the Western web. People mostly shrugged their shoulders when Egypt banned porn, because Egypt clamping down on its telecom industry isn't a big surprise. We don't stress about China's unending attempts to kill the internet because, hey, that's just what those power-hungry dudes in the Politburo do, and it's not really stopping anyone anyway.

But when Iceland, one of those progressive Nordic darlings that the *Economist* can't stop raving about, is thinking about knocking a whole bunch of the web offline, we ought to be concerned. Such a ban likely couldn't be copied in the US, where we still have some vestiges of the First Amendment, but Jonasson's proposal is just the latest piece of a trend towards Western nations regulating the web more strictly than they do other spaces.

Remember that the porn ban idea isn't new; the UK was wrestling with (and eventually denied) the idea last year. Porn is fighting its own battle in the US, but seems pretty safe for now online. Instead, we've got the return of CISPA [Cyber Intelligence Sharing and Protection Act], which still allows companies to disclose private user info to the government without warrants. We've also got such an asinine system for copyright protection online that everyone from NASA to Retraction Watch can have their own original content yanked off the web because someone else claimed it as their own.

Government Overreach

Iceland's proposed porn ban represents all of the recent problems with governments flexing control over the web: Officials don't understand how the Internet works—comparing a space launch to controlling and blocking diffused data on the web is asinine, I'm sorry—and they continue to think of "Internet users" as a discrete bloc of constituents that are all a bunch of basement-dwelling porn-addict pirates that wouldn't vote anyway.

The reality is that the Internet isn't the realm of a few savvy folks. It's used by everyone, even if officials ignore that. Designing wide-reaching legislation that bars access to large parts to the most important resource in existence today doesn't simply limit the people who *shouldn't be doing that bad stuff.*

Instead, because regulators don't understand how the laws they're passing work nor do they understand (or care) just how many citizens they're targeting, we end up with laws that have more unintended effects that intended. For example, if Iceland really does ban porn, it either won't block everything, or will block too much. The same goes for the DMCA [Digital Millennium Copyright Act], and doubly so for CISPA, where the threat of "internet terrorists"—whose correspondence isn't going to be tracked anyway—is paving the way for warrantless spying on just about anything you do online.

The fact is, there's simply no way to regulate the Internet with a scalpel. It's impossible, unless the answer is to bar all access to the Internet at large and replace it with a state-run intranet like Iran or North Korea. But lawmakers in the West increasingly seem to think that either they can, or more likely that citizens won't know or care enough to protest as the rights they'd expect IRL [in real life] disappear online.

Periodical and Internet Sources Bibliography

The following articles have been selected to supplement the diverse views presented in this chapter.

Dave Bohon	"Iceland Considers Pornography Ban—Why Not United States?," *New American*, February 25, 2013.
Jeff Carter	"Stop SOPA Now: Why It's Important to the Average Joe," Townhall, January 19, 2012. www.townhall.com.
Gloria Goodale	"SOPA and PIPA Bills: Old Answers to 21st-Century Problems, Critics Say," *Christian Science Monitor*, January 18, 2012.
Doug Gross	"Iceland Wants to Ban Internet Porn," CNN.com, February 15, 2013. www.cnn.com.
Andrew Leonard	"Internet Blackout!," *Salon*, January 18, 2012. www.salon.com.
Michael O'Leary	"Stop Protecting Criminal Behavior: Why Critics Are Wrong About the Stop Online Piracy Act," *Huffington Post*, December 15, 2011. www.huffingtonpost.com.
David Rohde	"China's Newest Export: Internet Censorship," Reuters, November 17, 2011. www.reuters.com.
Julian Sanchez	"SOPA: An Architecture for Censorship," Cato Institute, December 20, 2011. www.cato.org.
Pierce Stanley	"How SOPA Could Have Hindered Our Democracy Promotion Efforts," *New Republic*, January 21, 2012.
Nicci Talbot	"Can Iceland Ban Internet Porn?," *Huffington Post*, February 25, 2013. www.huffingtonpost.com.

For Further Discussion

Chapter 1

1. Should governments have the right to limit Internet access or censor the Internet? Cite from the first three viewpoints in the chapter to inform your answer.

2. In his viewpoint, Marc Thiessen considers WikiLeaks to be a national security threat that should be censored. Jillian York contends that the US government should not pressure US companies to censor WikiLeaks. Do you agree with the US government's attempts to force companies to censor WikiLeaks? Why or why not?

Chapter 2

1. In the past few years, the question of Internet governance has been a controversial issue. After reading the viewpoints in this chapter, what institution do you believe is best suited to govern the Internet? Which one do you believe would be the worst choice? Explain, citing from the viewpoints?

2. Milton L. Mueller argues that US control of the Internet is dangerous. Arthur Herman asserts that the United States is the best choice to ensure Internet freedom. Which author do you think makes the more persuasive argument? Why?

Chapter 3

1. This chapter examines several ways to fight against Internet censorship. After reading the viewpoints in the chapter, which method do you believe is the most effective in that fight? Which one do you think is the least effective? Why?

2. Paul Wiseman reports on the role of hacktivists in the battle for Internet freedom. How do you think hacktivists can benefit Internet freedom? Do you perceive a threat to Internet freedom from hacktivists? Explain your position.

Chapter 4

1. Cindy Cohn, Jillian C. York, and Trevor Timm assert that the Global Online Freedom Act (GOFA) provides sufficient protection against Internet censorship. In her viewpoint, Rebecca MacKinnon disagrees with that assessment, finding GOFA to be flawed and ineffective in protecting Internet freedom. In your opinion, which viewpoint makes the more persuasive and well-considered argument? Why?

2. The Stop Online Piracy Act (SOPA) has proved to be a controversial piece of legislation in the United States. Do you think it should be enacted? Cite from the viewpoints by Nancy Scola and Lamar Smith to inform your opinion.

3. Iceland's proposed ban on online violent pornography has caused global controversy. Halla Gunnarsdóttir believes such a ban is necessary to protect children and will not threaten Internet freedom. Derek Mead considers such a ban to be a form of Internet censorship. Which viewpoint do you agree with and why?

Organizations to Contact

The editors have compiled the following list of organizations concerned with the issues debated in this book. The descriptions are derived from materials provided by the organizations. All have publications or information available for interested readers. The list was compiled on the date of publication of the present volume; names, addresses, phone and fax numbers, and email and Internet addresses may change. Be aware that many organizations take several weeks or longer to respond to inquiries, so allow as much time as possible.

Electronic Frontier Foundation (EFF)
454 Shotwell Street, San Francisco, CA   94110
(415) 436-9333 • fax: (415) 436-9993
email: info@eff.org
website: www.eff.org

The Electronic Frontier Foundation was established in 1990 to protect the rights of individuals and businesses in cyberspace from government interference and persecution. To that end, the EFF takes on legal cases to set precedents on the issue of Internet freedom and confirm the rights of individuals and business in cyberspace. Over the years, the EFF has come to address emerging threats to Internet freedom from industry, especially in the area of copyright law. Another project of the EFF is the fight for privacy on the Internet, particularly in situations where governments monitor Internet communications in the interest of national security. The EFF informs hackers, whistleblowers, and anyone on the Internet of their rights under the law and offers assistance to anyone under government suspicion or surveillance. The organization's website has a range of information on topical issues, including hacking, privacy, innovation, copyright law, and bloggers' rights. It also hosts a blog that covers recent events and research, breaking news, upcoming EFF initiatives and legal cases, and relevant policies all over the world.

Fight for the Future

PO Box 55071 #95005, Boston, MA   02205
(508) 474-5248
email: team@fightforthefuture.org
website: www.fightforthefuture.org

Fight for the Future is an activist organization developing "a grassroots movement to ensure that everyone can access the Internet's many resources affordably, free of interference and with full privacy." Fight for the Future collaborates with colleagues in the nonprofit sector and technology industry to protect Internet freedom. One recent and successful viral campaign was launched to inform the public about the dangers of the Stop Online Piracy Act (SOPA), which was being debated in the US Congress. The organization's website provides information on its latest campaigns and initiatives and offers information to the public on a number of complicated issues such as copyright and patent laws, Internet censorship legislation, and cybertracking and cybertheft.

Free Press

40 Main Street, Suite 301, Florence, MA   01062
(877) 888-1533
website: www.freepress.net

Free Press (not to be confused with the New York publishing house of the same name) is an organization that was created to fight for "universal and affordable Internet access, diverse media ownership, vibrant public media and quality journalism." It works for this goal through public education, grassroots activism, research, and public advocacy. Free Press also created the SavetheInternet.com coalition, a viral movement dedicated to preserving Internet freedom and fighting against censorship and legislation to limit access to the Internet. One of its current campaigns pushes for universal access to high-speed Internet across the United States. The group's website features information about that campaign and others, and also has a blog and educational tools for aspiring activists.

International Telecommunication Union (ITU)

Place des Nations, Geneva 20   1211
  Switzerland
+41 22 730 5111 • fax: +41 22 733 7256
email: itumail@itu.int
website: www.itu.int

The International Telecommunication Union is a specialized agency of the United Nations that deals with information and communications technologies. The ITU allocates global radio spectrum and satellite orbits, develops technical standards that allow for the interconnection of networks and technologies, and works to enhance access to modern communications technology for people all over the world. The ITU views Internet access as a basic human right and strives to provide that access to underserved areas in developing countries. The ITU publishes a range of information, including statistics, online reports, and the e-newsletter *ITU News*. The website features a news blog and calendar of upcoming events, including youth summits and conferences.

Internet Corporation for Assigned Names and Numbers (ICANN)

12025 Waterford Drive, Suite 300, Los Angeles, CA   90094
(310) 301-5800 • fax: (301) 823-8649
website: www.icann.org

ICANN is a nonprofit organization that plays an important role in managing the Internet: it coordinates the global Internet system; preserves the Internet's operational stability; and develops policies to keep the Internet competitive, growing, and open. In other words, much of the technical coordination and maintenance of the global Internet system is the responsibility of this organization. To educate the public about technical aspects of how the Internet works and ICANN's mission, the group's website features a number of informational materials, including podcasts, webinars, audio briefings, fact sheets, and guidebooks.

National Counterterrorism Center (NCTC)
Office of the Director of National Intelligence
Washington, DC   20511
(703) 733-8600
website: www.nctc.gov

An agency of the Office of the Director of National Intelligence (DNI), the National Counterterrorism Center analyzes emerging and existing threats to the safety of the United States, disseminates relevant intelligence with other government agencies and partners, develops operational strategies, and marshals the resources of the national government to address those threats effectively. The NCTC also advises the DNI on intelligence analysis and operations relating to counterterrorism and serves as the central resource for all information on counterterrorism activities and intelligence. On the NCTC website can be found press releases, interviews, speeches, and testimony from NCTC officials, published reports, fact sheets, and the legislation that established the center. There is also a NCTC kids page, which offers children an introduction to the NCTC and its activities.

National Cyber Security Division (NCSD)
Twelfth & C Streets SW, Washington, DC   20024
(202) 282-8000
website: www.dhs.gov/national-cyber-security-division

The National Cyber Security Division is a division of the Department of Homeland Security that focuses on protecting American national security in cyberspace. The NCSD coordinates public, private, and international entities to secure American assets; monitors and analyzes cyberthreats; and maintains the National Cyber Alert System, which informs public and private entities of potential cyberattacks. NCSD maintains the US-CERT system, which recognizes threats and coordinates response strategies. It also coordinates the Cyber Storm, an international cybersecurity exercise to test the response to a catastrophic cyberattack.

National Security Agency/Central Security Service (NSA/CSS)

9800 Savage Road, Fort Meade, MD   20755
(301) 688-6524 • fax: (301) 688-6198
email: nsapao@nsa.gov
website: www.nsa.gov

The National Security Agency/Central Security Service is a partnership between two premier US security organizations: The NSA offers timely foreign policy analysis for US political and military leaders, and the CSS provides cryptological knowledge and assistance and develops policies for the national-security community. One of the organization's key missions is Information Assurance, a strategy to prevent foreign countries and individual hackers from gaining access to classified national security information and to shore up vulnerabilities in America's cybersecurity. The NSA/CSS website offers access to recent press releases and breaking news, transcripts of speeches and testimony of NSA/CSS staff, and *The Next Wave*, an agency journal that publishes in-depth articles, commentary, and research.

Public Knowledge

1818 N Street NW, Suite 410, Washington, DC   20036
(202) 861-0020 • fax: (202) 861-0040
email: pk@publicknowledge.org
website: www.publicknowledge.org

Public Knowledge is an organization that "preserves the openness of the Internet and the public's access to knowledge, promotes creativity through balanced copyright, and upholds and protects the rights of consumers to use innovative technology lawfully." It strives to protect universal access to a safe and affordable Internet by opposing governmental and corporate attempts to censor content or limit access. One of its main efforts is in education, and it publishes papers, studies, editorials, and other materials to inform the public of threats to Internet freedom. This material can be accessed on the organization's website, which also features a blog, videos, and podcasts that explore breaking news and relevant topics.

US Department of Homeland Security (DHS)
Twelfth & C Streets SW, Washington, DC   20024
(202) 282-8000
website: www.dhs.gov

The Department of Homeland Security is tasked with protecting the United States from terrorist attacks and other threats. Established after the terrorist attacks of September 11, 2001, the DHS aims to reduce the vulnerability of US infrastructure and installations, government officials, and major events to attacks of any kind; to enforce and administer immigration laws to better control who is traveling in and out of the country; to coordinate and administer the national response to terrorist attacks and be a key player in recovery and rebuilding efforts; and to safeguard and secure cyberspace by assessing cyber-threats and coordinating a counterattack. The DHS works closely with other government agencies and relevant partners to protect the nation's cybersecurity. The DHS website allows access to a number of informative resources, including fact sheets, breaking news, press releases, speeches and testimony of DHS officials, videos, and other publications on topics of interest.

Bibliography of Books

Charles Beckett
with James Ball

WikiLeaks: News in the Networked Era. Cambridge, UK: Polity Press, 2012.

Joel Brenner

America the Vulnerable: Inside the New Threat Matrix of Digital Espionage, Crime, and Warfare. New York: Penguin, 2011.

Christopher
Coker

Warrior Geeks: How 21st-Century Technology Is Changing the Way We Fight and Think About War. New York: Columbia University Press, 2012.

Gabriella
Coleman

Coding Freedom: The Ethics and Aesthetics of Hacking. Princeton, NJ: Princeton University Press, 2012.

John David Ebert

The New Media Invasion: Digital Technologies and the World They Unmake. Jefferson, NC: McFarland, 2011.

Richard Fontaine
and Will Rogers

Internet Freedom: A Foreign Policy Imperative in the Digital Age. Washington, DC: Center for a New American Security, 2011.

Andrew Fowler

The Most Dangerous Man in the World: The Explosive True Story of Julian Assange and the Lies, Cover-ups, and Conspiracies He Exposed. New York: Skyhorse, 2013.

Andrew Greenberg	*This Machine Kills Secrets: How WikiLeakers, Cypherpunks, and Hacktivists Aim to Free the World's Information.* New York: Dutton, 2012.
George K. Kostopoulos	*Cyberspace and Cybersecurity.* Boca Raton, FL: CRC Press, 2013.
David Leigh and Luke Harding	*WikiLeaks: Inside Julian Assange's War on Secrecy.* New York: Public Affairs, 2011.
Saul Levmore and Martha Craven Nussbaum, eds.	*The Offensive Internet: Speech, Privacy, and Reputation.* Cambridge, MA: Harvard University Press, 2010.
Rebecca MacKinnon	*Consent of the Networked: The Worldwide Struggle for Internet Freedom.* New York: Basic Books, 2012.
Robert McChesney	*Digital Disconnect: How Capitalism Is Turning the Internet Against Democracy.* New York: New Press, 2013.
Nicco Mele	*The End of Big: How the Internet Makes David the New Goliath.* New York: St. Martin's, 2013.
Evgeny Morozov	*The Net Delusion: The Dark Side of Internet Freedom.* New York: Public Affairs, 2011.
Jason Q. Ng	*Blocked on Weibo: What Gets Suppressed on China's Version of Twitter (and Why).* New York: New Press, 2013.

Denver Nicks — *Private: Bradley Manning, WikiLeaks, and the Biggest Exposure of Official Secrets in American History.* Chicago: Chicago Review Press, 2012.

Parmy Olson — *We Are Anonymous: Inside the Hacker World of Lulzsec, Anonymous, and the Global Cyber Conspiracy.* New York: Little, Brown, 2012.

Kevin Poulsen — *Kingpin: How One Hacker Took Over the Billion-Dollar Cybercrime Underground.* New York: Crown, 2011.

Derek S. Reveron, ed. — *Cyberspace and National Security: Threats, Opportunities, and Power in a Virtual World.* Washington, DC: Georgetown University Press, 2012.

Paul Rosenzweig — *Cyber Warfare: How Conflicts in Cyberspace Are Challenging America and Changing the World.* Santa Barbara, CA: Praeger, 2012.

Daniel J. Solove — *Nothing to Hide: The False Tradeoff Between Privacy and Security.* New Haven, CT: Yale University Press, 2011.

Robert Zelnick and Eva Zelnick — *The Illusion of Net Neutrality: Political Alarmism, Regulatory Creep, and the Real Threat to Internet Freedom.* Stanford, CA: Hoover Institution Press, 2013.

Index

CPSIA information can be obtained
at www.ICGtesting.com
Printed in the USA
FFOW03n0133200315
12018FF

9 780737 766592